ON WINGS LIKE EAGLES

LAMAR DODSON

Lost Coast Press

Fort Bragg, California

On Wings Like Eagles

For information or to order additional copies, please contact:

Lost Coast Press
155 Cypress Street
Fort Bragg, CA 95437
(800) 773-7782
Fax (707) 964-7531

Library of Congress Cataloging-in-Publication Data

Dodson, Lamar.
On wings like eagles / Lamar Dodson.
p. cm.
ISBN No. 1-882897-16-1
I. Title.
PS3554.034305 1997
813'.54—dc21 97-19249
CIP

Bible quotations from the New International Version.
Eagle illustration on cover by Paula Teplitz
Handwritten notes on cover by Salinas Christian School
Eighth Grade class

First Edition, June 1997

2 4 6 8 10 9 7 5 3 1

Printed in Canada

ON WINGS LIKE EAGLES

Dedication

In memory of my son Danny

(December 29, 1968 to November 23, 1992)

CONTENTS

CHAPTER ONE

FLASHBACK

But those who hope in the LORD *will renew their strength. They will soar on wings like eagles; they will run and not grow weary, they will walk and not be faint.*
—Isaiah 40:31

I will not cry. I will not cry. I will not cry.

Easy to say!

Graduation. I can't believe I made it! It's an awesome feeling sitting on this stage surrounded by my classmates and staring into the sea of faces all poised to share this momentous occasion with us. Some of us in this class have been together at John Mark Christian School for eleven years. Yeah, that's right. We had two years of pre-school before we even began kindergarten. That was so very, very long ago. So much has happened. I guess if you are as old as Miss Puffer, the sixth grade teacher, the account of our brief lives would be like a tiny pimple on your face by comparison.

Mr. Cooper, my Bible teacher, says it's okay for guys to cry. I don't know about that. I've never seen my dad shed a tear.

Theresa is singing right now. I hope she doesn't start crying like she did during practice this morning. She's singing "Pray for Me" while facing us and focusing all of her attention on us. She's so-o-o cool for a girl, that is.

I'll never forget the first time I met Theresa. It was last August just before this school year began. Theresa and her sixth grade brother were with their mother to register as new students. Under normal conditions I would be as far from school as possible with only one week to go before opening day. Pastor Bob, our youth pastor, had asked my dad if he could borrow a few of our puppets, so I was on a mission to deliver the puppets to him. I stuffed the puppets into my backpack, jumped on my bike, and headed for school. As I pedaled along Acorn Street, I had to hold one of the puppets, a gorilla, because it wouldn't fit in the backpack. Ever the clown, I used the gorilla to entertain both myself and the passing motorists. While stopped at a red light about a block from the school, a new Ford Taurus station wagon pulled up beside me. Theresa sat in the front on the passenger side. Of course I had no idea who she was at the time. She stared intently at Adam, my gorilla friend, and then laughing, turned to say something to her mother. Seizing the opportunity, I let out a few high-pitched gorilla sounds, had Adam gyrate around, and lunge in Theresa's direction. When the light changed and as the station wagon pulled away, Theresa made a face and stuck out her tongue at me. That was the longest tongue I had ever seen. It was "hate at first sight." Who did she think she was? I was funny. Why, most of the time people laughed and threw money in my direction. Well, it did happen once.

You can imagine my surprise when I walked into the office toting a gorilla, a blonde-haired female puppet which we had named Eve, and an assortment of birds and reptiles in my backpack and came face to face with "the tongue."

I would have walked by without saying a word, but Mrs. Nelson, the secretary, said, "Oh, PJ, wait a moment. I'd like you to meet Theresa and her brother, Bryan. Theresa will be in your class this year."

I slowed down, looked in their direction, and as instant recognition set in, ducked my head. "Oh, no! My worst nightmare!" I exclaimed.

Theresa laughed. "I think we've already met. Well, sorta.

Which one of you is PJ?" she asked, pointing first at the dummies and then at me.

She and her brother laughed so loudly Mrs. Nelson gave them a funny look.

She could definitely market that laugh, I thought.

"Am I missing something? What's the joke?" Mrs. Nelson asked.

Theresa's mother, Mrs. Gassett, came to my rescue. "This young man entertained us with his puppets while we were stopped at a red light on the way here," she stated. "He was very funny."

"Not!" I said, trying to cover my embarrassment.

"Well, I gotta go. See ya."

I was out of there. And that was my introduction to Theresa.

Lots of stuff happened this year. As I sit here reflecting back on the year, I realize what a major role Theresa has played. Right now she's singing to a class that hated her during the first half of the year. In a few minutes she'll be giving the valedictory speech. Who would have thought that Theresa could overcome all of the obstacles thrown in her way to accomplish what she has this year? I must admit, I was one of her worst enemies, and it took me until Christmas to turn it around. Our school emblem is the golden eagle, and we have Isaiah 40:31 drilled into our heads. Theresa has not only learned the verse mentally but also has put it into practice.

The day she intercepted the glider I launched toward Gus is a day that will forever live in infamy. They will talk about that event in the halls of John Mark Christian School for years to come. Theresa was instrumental in getting the first prayer group going this year. The school finally organized a student council, and Theresa served as President. I'll always remember the Christmas program where Theresa and I surprised everyone by singing a duet. But you've heard most of this stuff in that other book. Now, as Paul Harvey says, "It's time for you to hear the rest of the story."

CHAPTER TWO

A TIME FOR EVERYTHING

There is a time for everything, and a season for every activity under the sun.

— Ecclesiastes 3:1

Kent asked me to come over to his place to listen to a new tape he got for Christmas. I had been out of school for a week and was already bored with the daily routine of arguing with my little sister, practicing for a puppet show with my dad, shooting hoops, jogging with Jezi (our dachshund), and just lolling around. Winter Camp was coming up, but that was two weeks away. So, Kent's invitation was a welcome relief from monotony.

Kent lives about a mile from my house, so I had time as I pedaled along to think about how he and Dawn were expelled from John Mark Christian School last November. After we patched things up between us at the 10K Christmas run, I hadn't seen him for awhile. I guess I secretly felt somewhat responsible for what happened, although I knew deep down in my heart I wasn't. Kent and Dawn brought it on themselves when they sneaked off at camp and were caught making out. Mr. Cramer, our principal, assured me that what I told him about them cheating on the history test had absolutely nothing to do with his decision to expel them.

Kent occasionally comes to youth group on Tuesday night, but he's not much into it. I think he only comes because of the girls, or "babes" as he calls them. In my opinion, he should take school more seriously and leave the babes alone. There's a time for everything, and this is not the time to mess with girls at least not up close and personal. The "daylight" rule is strictly enforced at John Mark and knowing what the punishment would be is a strong deterrent to help us keep our hands off. Admiring them from a distance is my motto. Secretly, I guess I was just jealous. Loud music was blaring, and I wondered if it was coming from Kent's house. I already knew the answer.

My friendship with Kent dates way back to pre-school. He's always been a rather strange duck, and although I don't like to admit it, much of the serious trouble in my life can be directly attributable to him. In the second grade we got caught sneaking into an "R-rated" movie. The theater manager called our parents, and I had trouble sitting down for a few days after that if you know what I mean. In fourth grade a neighbor reported us to the police for shooting at birds with our BB guns. I don't remember that we actually ever hit one, but the police made a federal case of it and instructed my parents to keep me under control or I would end up in juvenile hall. I didn't know what that was at the time, but it scared me so badly I got on my knees and asked God to forgive me and keep me from that awful place. In fifth grade we both got binoculars for Christmas. We had great fun spying on everyone. Actually, I was so ashamed of some of the things I saw with those binoculars, I hid them and told Kent they were broken. I must admit, however, that the very worst thing I was involved with I did all by my lonesome. Our family went to Honolulu one summer where we stayed on the fourteenth floor of this really neat hotel. One afternoon after I had just gone for a swim, I returned to the room to shower and get dressed for dinner. I was alone. I filled a glass with ice, got a coke, and stood on the balcony watching all the people pass by on the street below. I remember that they looked like ants. Then I did a really stupid thing. I began pelting "the ants" with ice from my glass. Well, let me tell you, before you could say "Jack Robinson" a security guard was in my face and had me pushed up against the balcony wall. How he figured out which room the ice was coming from and how he got there so fast are two questions I'll want answered when I get to heaven, and I do plan to get there. To make a long story short, my parents were advised that one more incident was all it would take for us to be permanently banned from that hotel (and from the islands if they had anything to say about it).

My thoughts were interrupted as I turned the corner onto Kent's street. The music was even more deafening. Kent lives in an older, two-story house in a rather run-down neighborhood. Don't remind him of that though. It's a real sore spot. He lived across the street from me until his dad split. Then his mother had to sell the house because they could no longer afford it.

I locked my bike to the tetherball pole on the side of the house as usual and, cupping my hands around my mouth, yelled, "Kent!"

"Yeah, man, come on up," he yelled back, sticking his head out the screenless window.

"Can you turn the music down?" I shouted.

"What?"

"The music. Turn it down," I said, role-playing as if I were turning a knob.

"Oh, yeah, sure, dude! No problem. Get yourself on up here."

Kent was home alone which wasn't that unusual. His parents were divorced, and he lived with his mother who worked full time and two older brothers. The house was a mess, but then I'm not a neatnik myself and certainly no judge of tidiness. Kent was throwing stuff into a closet when I entered the room.

"This place is a mess, dude!" he exclaimed.

That's the understatement of the century, I thought, but I just smiled and nodded. At least he had turned the stereo down so the walls were no longer vibrating.

"Sit on the bed there . . . just shove that stuff out of the way. I'm glad you came. I was getting real bored, man," he said.

"Yeah, me too. My sister was driving me bonkers. She's such a spoiled little brat, and I have to put up with her for one more week of vacation."

"How do you like it?" he asked, pointing to the stereo.

"That song is by Motley Crue. It's called 'Shout at the Devil'," he commented. "I got two other tapes that are even better."

I nodded, but said nothing.

I knew Kent liked heavy rock music, but this stuff was way far out. I couldn't believe what my ears were hearing. If my parents caught me listening to music like this, they would send me away to some military school in Iceland. I was surprised the neighbors hadn't called the police about the noise much less the words. The music Kent listens to explains a lot about the way he acts and talks. Even his vocabulary has deteriorated to the point where he can hardly complete a sentence without using profanity. He knows how I feel about that, so at least he tones the language down when I'm around.

"Say, after you hear my other tapes, we can go to the Arcade and play video games. Okay?" Kent asked.

"Sounds good to me, man. I have around ten bucks."

I wanted to get away from that music. On the floor by the stereo there were cassettes by Pink Floyd, Kiss, Mr. Mister, and Def Leppard. I wanted no part of it. A couple of Playboy magazines lay at my feet beside the bed. On the wall above the bed a pretty suntanned girl in a skimpy bikini lay sunbathing on the beach.

What happened? How could this guy have changed so much? Almost overnight it seems that our lives had changed dramatically. I was thinking about keeping my grades up, about college, and about serving God while these things seemed to be the farthest from his mind.

"Why don't we listen to the tapes later. I need to get back to the house by 1:00 to help my mom," I said.

Kent was rummaging through the pockets of a pair of jeans, let out a string of curse words, and threw the pants down forcefully. "Wait 'til I get my hands on that creep. I'll tear him apart," he yelled.

"What're you talking about?" I asked.

"My stupid brother, man. He must've taken the money I had. It's okay. Come on. I know where I can get some money," he said, motioning for me to follow him out of the room.

He raced down the stairs two at a time and headed for the kitchen. As I entered the room, a drawer was open and Kent was taking some money out of a manila envelope.

"Dang, there's only a few bucks here," he said. "My mom must've paid the rent already."

"You're taking your mom's money?" I asked dumbfounded. "Isn't that stealing?"

"Nah. She won't miss it. Besides, she'll think one of my brothers took it. They'll get into a big argument and everyone will be blamed, but I'm the baby of the family so I get away with lots of stuff."

He stuffed the money into his jeans, and we headed out the back door.

I knew it was pointless to argue with Kent about honesty, and I didn't really have the courage to confront him. Kent could clean my plate without blinking an eye if I pushed him. I knew he professed to be a Christian, but I wondered how he could rationalize using profanity, listening to Satanic music, reading pornographic magazines, and stealing from his mother — all of which I had personally witnessed in the past few minutes — with being a Christian. I decided to keep the peace and let God send another prophet to convey His "woe-unto-you" message to Kent. Maybe that's the way Jonah felt when God asked him to go preach to the sinners in Ninevah, I reasoned. Jonah was swallowed by a humongous fish for not listening to God. This is different though. It really isn't any of my business. It's neither the time nor the place to play preacher-boy.

We were approaching Washington Junior High where Kent and Dawn go to school. It was like Kent was reading my mind because he said, "That religion stuff just doesn't seem to work for me. I go to youth group and I try to pray, but God doesn't answer. I guess I'm a loser. What's the use. Life doesn't seem to have much purpose. Sometimes I just want to end it all."

"Don't even kid around about things like that, man," I countered. "I can't tell you how to live your life, but I know believing in God makes all the difference. If you really trust in Him, He will be there for you."

"Sure, sure! That's easy for you to say, PJ. Your dad and mom make a good home for you. You have money, make good grades, and everybody likes you. I have to fight for everything. My dad walked out, my brothers hassle me, my mom hates me, and I got kicked out of John Mark. Now I have to attend this dumb school (pointing to Washington) with all the gangs and teachers who don't care beans for you. I haven't got a friend in the world there."

I didn't say anything, and we rode on in silence. We turned the corner, and I followed Kent as he maneuvered his bike to jump the curb. We rode single-file until we arrived at the shopping mall. We locked our bikes in the bike rack outside the video store and went inside. After exchanging a dollar bill for some tokens, I played Defender, one of my favorite video games. On a good day I could make one token last for over an hour and come up with a score high enough to qualify me as the top scorer of record. Kent was playing a game called Asteroids. Once I heard him curse and bang on the machine. I noticed later that he was moving from game to game which meant he was going through tokens rather quickly.

"I'm going out for a few minutes, PJ. I'll be right back. Don't leave without me," he said, putting his hand on my shoulder.

"Hey, where are you going? Wait 'til I finish, and I'll go with you," I said, thinking he was going to get something to eat. I love to eat more than anything in the world, and my stomach was letting me know it was about time to fill the cavity.

"No, honest, I'm just going to Target to get something. When I come back, we can go to McD's for burgers 'n' fries. I'll let you buy me lunch, okay?" He was gone before I could answer.

It wasn't a good day for me. I had already blown a dollar and half of the tokens from a $3.00 coupon special I bought. I switched to a game called Turbo and was on it for so long I forgot the time.

Where was Kent, I wondered? He had been gone for about forty-five minutes. I finished my game and walked outside. Shielding my eyes from the bright sun, I looked left and right to see if I could spot Kent. Our bikes were still locked where we had left them. As I walked toward Target, I got a funny feeling in my stomach. I noticed a police car parked at the curb. I tried to remember

Kent's exact words when he left. Did he say, "I'm going to pick something up?" I know he was broke, so there was no way he could be buying something.

CHAPTER THREE

THE WRITING ON THE WALL

Suddenly the fingers of a human hand appeared and on the plaster of the wall . . .

— Daniel 5:5

I stood there in shock and disbelief as I saw Kent emerge from the store with a policeman at his side. Kent was ushered into the back seat by the officer who quickly got into the patrol unit and drove away. It wasn't difficult for me to imagine what had transpired. I guess Kent thought he was above the law, or that he was so cool he wouldn't get caught. I am aware that sometimes when he goes shopping he changes the price tag of a high-priced item for one with a lower price. I know for a fact he did that with a tennis racket. He walked out of the store with a $150 racket and paid only $30 for it. I reminded him of the sophisticated detection devices and undercover sales clerks that stores employ to catch shoplifters, but he just laughed it off.

I didn't feel much like eating. Dejectedly, I unlocked my bike and headed for home.

"Where ya been, big brother?" asked Patti. She and my mom were having lunch together on the patio.

"What's it to ya?" I responded.

"Whoa, what's with the attitude, PJ?" asked Mom.

I didn't respond but sat down at the table cupping my head between my hands.

"Want to tell us about it?" queried my mom.

"Can I talk to you alone, Mom?" I asked.

"Sure, hon. Patti, why don't you take your sandwich in the kitchen and finish it? You can start doing the dishes, too, and I'll be in to help you in a second."

"Aah, Mom, can't I stay and listen? I'd like to hear about the trouble PJ is into now. His life is better than a soap opera," said Patti. But she obediently picked up her stuff, stuck out her tongue at me, and huffed off toward the house.

My mom is a good listener. I quickly related the events of the morning to her.

"What should I do?" I asked.

"Well, son, there's really not much you can do to help Kent at this point. Pray for him," she said, patting my hand and looking at me sympathetically. "I'll call Pastor Bob. He'll know what to do."

I knew Mom was right.

I learned later that Kent spent the day in juvenile hall and was released to his mom that evening. He would have to be in court to appear before a judge who would determine his punishment. I didn't see Kent until the next week at youth group. He and Gus were talking to Janelle and Diana when I walked up. "I can't wait," Diana was saying.

"Wait for what?" I asked.

"Winter camp, dude. It's going to be a blast!" she exclaimed.

"I got new snow boots for Christmas," volunteered Janelle.

"I hope you get a chance to use them. Remember last year? There wasn't any snow. That camp was a dud. I don't know if I want to waste my time with it this year," said Gus.

"Okay, but you'll miss out, bud. Pastor Bob has a really neat music group coming this year. The speaker's going to be awesome, and the girls! Why, you won't find a finer bunch of beauties anywhere," teased Janelle.

"Not," I said.

I noticed that Kent wasn't really getting into the conversation.

In fact, he was looking away, so I asked, "Are you going this year, Kent?"

He gave me a quizzical look, like I of all people should know better, and said sarcastically, "Nah, I have to be somewhere else."

I realized that probably no one else knew about the shoplifting incident, and this wasn't a good time to bring it up, so I changed the subject.

"Gus, come with me and let's find out from Pastor Bob what's going on tonight," I said.

Sometimes youth group is really fun. Absolutely the best part is just hanging out with your friends. We always try to get other kids from our class to come on Tuesday nights, but most of them give the excuse that they don't have time because of all the homework we have to do.

After we sang a few choruses, we got really hyped when Pastor Bob announced that the entertainment for the evening would be a couple of movies, "The Cat Came Back" and "Bambi vs. Godzilla". Most of us have seen these cartoons a zillion times but never grow tired of watching them.

We yelled and screamed and went crazy for the next hour. It was fun. The evening ended on a serious note as Pastor Bob talked to us about righteousness. That's a big word, but all it really means is doing the right things for the right reasons. We've certainly heard *that* definition enough to know it by heart. I don't have the foggiest idea how to practice it though.

Kent came up to me after the meeting and said, "I don't appreciate the way you embarrassed me in front of everybody, PJ."

"What're you talking about, Kent? What did I do?" I asked.

"Like you don't know, already. You were trying to get me to talk about my trouble with the police, weren't you?" He was pushing me backwards with every word he said.

Lucky for me, Pastor Bob came along.

"Hey, guys, let's pile into the bus (meaning his van) and go get some hot chocolate," he said, putting one arm around Kent and one around me and shoving us forward.

I made it a point to stay far away from Kent for the rest of the evening and made sure Pastor Bob took me home first.

After Christmas break, to my absolute amazement the school was still there. I walked into the classroom with my backpack loaded with books which I hadn't even taken out over the holidays.

Mr. Cooper, I noticed, hadn't aged a bit in the past two weeks. He was reading his Bible while rubbing what little hair he had left at the top of his forehead. Maggie had a running joke going with Mr. Cooper about his lack of hair. She would say, "Have you fallen over backwards and hit your forehead lately, Mr. Cooper?"

It was a sick joke and she got all giggly about it, but Mr. Cooper seemed to take it in stride.

Mr. Cooper acknowledged my presence, asked me how my vacation was, and continued reading. I unloaded my backpack and began working on the ten pages of math which were supposed to be done and ready to check by math time. Woe is me, I thought. I'll never get all of this done. I should have finished it during vacation. Other kids started to arrive, and then Mrs. Nelson walked into our room with a new girl.

"Mr. Cooper, this is Lori Johnson.

She's going to be in your class," said the secretary.

"I'm glad to meet you, Lori. Let's see where we can find a place for you," he said, looking at his seating chart.

"I'd like very much to sit near the front, Sir, if that's possible," she said.

"Sir? Sir!" Nobody called the teacher "sir". What's with this girl? I noticed that the corrective lens in Lori's glasses were very thick. Uh-oh, she's going to be in for lots of teasing, I thought.

"From your accent I'd say you're from the South. How far off am I if I guess Texas?" asked Mr. Cooper.

"Why, how'd ya know that, Sir?" she said sweetly.

This conversation was not helping me finish my math, so I left while Lori was being fitted for a desk and getting all of her books. I had picked up a cold over vacation, and my nose was running like it was trying to win a marathon or something. Since there is never any kleenex in our room, I walked to the restroom to get some toilet tissue to blow my nose. After blowing my nose, I took a roll of partially-used paper and stuffed it in my jacket pocket to use during the day.

The boys' restroom is generally a mess. The stench is almost unbearable. I've tried going all day without using the facility, but with my bladder that's an impossibility; besides, leaving the room to visit the "john" is necessary to protect your sanity when things heat up. Paper towels are strewn about, the sinks are dirty, ugly black scuff marks decorate the tile floor, and some free-lance artist thinks the wall by the sinks is his private mural. Whoever the artist is, he isn't easily discouraged. The custodians diligently repaint the marred area almost on a weekly basis. Actually, I use the word "artist" loosely because the dude is badly in need of lessons. The writing on the wall is so crudely scratched I sometimes wonder if the author is coding an apocalyptic message to post a warning about teachers or ominous events yet to be. One thing is sure. It won't be long before Mr. Cramer sends out an all-points bulletin to catch the offender, and I would hate to be in that dude's shoes on judgment day. I came into the room juggling that partially used roil of toilet tissue and a partially-eaten apple. It seems the clown in me just refuses to die. No one even noticed. Everyone was chattering about presents received for Christmas, trips taken, sleeping in, and how much they hated being back at school. Being in a room with seventeen girls (actually it's eighteen now with Lori) and just six guys, we fellows have to put up with a lot. There's all the usual girl talk about hairdos, make-up (which is a no-no at John Mark), clothes, and all these cute guys that light up the girls' lives. Funny how they never talk about the guys in our room in a romantic way. I wonder what those other guys have that we don't have? Maybe they have hair under their arms, shave, and use some kind of exotic phoo-phoo.

At devotions it was like the chapel was full of zombies. Everyone was so quiet Mr. Cramer had a difficult time getting even the fifth and sixth graders to sing. Definitely not the norm. It's weird, but I have had this urge since about fifth grade to stand up right in the middle of the most somber moment and do my gorilla sounds.

Not a good idea. We are usually so rowdy that Mr. Cramer finally strikes his serious pose with his arms folded, his feet firmly planted, and with a stern look on his face in order to get us to be quiet. He gave up on the rowdy songs and led us in a few serious choruses. Before dismissing us, Mr. Cramer announced that a new student council was going to be formed. He presented the guidelines for those wanting to run for president, vice president, secretary, treasurer, and spiritual leader. He directed those interested to see their teacher for more information. I could see the banner now, "Vote for Peter Jonathan Nichols, III for President." That'll be the day, especially with my 2.6 grade point average.

During language arts Mr. Cooper was in rare form as he plunged like a madman into the depths of English grammar by demonstrating the complexities of sentence structure containing the regular subject–verb–complement pattern with the addition of adverb and adjective clauses. Of course his favorite way to demonstrate was by the use of sentence diagramming.

"And now, class, I will show you the mother of all diagrams," said Mr. Cooper, bowing and giving us a big smile. He turned to draw the diagram pattern on the board in the midst of groans and moans from everyone in the room except Lori.

"When will we ever use this stuff?" asked Gus.

"About the same time you'll use the algebraic equations you learn in math, Gus," offered Mr. Cooper. "You never know when someone will walk up to you and ask you to diagram a sentence. Why, just the other day, I was in Safeway and, wouldn't you know, the checker told me he would take twenty-five dollars off my receipt if I would diagram a sentence for him."

"Yeah, sure, Mr. Cooper. Now see what you've done, Gus. Mr. Cooper won't get off this horse for weeks," Maggie groaned.

"Well, you know my most favorite thing in the whole world to do is diagramming. During vacation I was able to diagram 1,215 sentences in a single day. I'll tell you what, I'll give anyone who successfully diagrams all the sentences I'm assigning for homework a dozen of my wife's famous chocolate chip cookies. Now that's a deal you can't beat," he said.

"No, really, Mr. Cooper, what you mean is that's a deal we can't eat," teased Theresa.

We all had vivid memories of the sugar cookies Mr. Cooper's wife had shared with us earlier in the year. It's hard to believe anyone could mess up a batch of sugar cookies, but as I looked around the room, I could tell by the grimaced faces that memories of the event would not soon be forgotten. It had become a joke which Mr. Cooper used to great advantage. Our standard reply to situations like the above was, "No, not the cookies, Mr. Cooper . . . anything but the cookies!"

I had to blow my nose so often during the morning that I finally left the roll of tissue on top of my desk. It was there when we took our mid-morning break, but when I came back to my desk it was gone.

"Very funny, PJ, very funny!" exclaimed Theresa, who suddenly appeared at my side towering over me like a giant buzzard.

"What're you talking about, girl?" I asked.

"You know very well what I'm talking about," shouted Theresa.

She lifted her desk top and revealed to the world a desk crammed full of wadded-up toilet tissue. Several books, pens, and pencils were neatly wrapped with tissue, and a tidy little bow completed the picture.

I must admit it was a funny sight, but I was sufficiently in control of my faculties to realize my predicament. If I laughed, I was dog meat. It didn't matter that the whole class was in stitches. Even Mr. Cooper who had come over to survey the scene was having a great deal of difficulty controlling his emotions.

"I've heard of teepeeing houses but I've never seen anything like this. This has got to be a first. We should make a video of what goes on in this class and sell it to make money for our Washington trip," Hunt announced.

"All right, Theresa, calm down. PJ, we all know you had the roll of tissue on your desk. Confession is good for the soul. If you come clean now, we can proceed with more important matters," stated Mr. Cooper.

"But I didn't do it, Mr. Cooper, honest, I didn't," I said, looking forlornly at him and then at Theresa.

"Sure, give me one reason why I should believe you," said Theresa, standing defiantly with her hands on her hips.

"That's one sure way to get a girl's attention," said Billy.

"Yea! The clown is back," shouted Sybil.

Oh, no, major deja vu, I thought. How am I going to get out of this one?

CHAPTER FOUR

AN ACCIDENT WAITING TO HAPPEN

Even a fool is thought wise if he keeps silent.
— Proverbs 17:27

"Look, Theresa, would I teepee your desk when everyone in the room knows I had that roll of tissue? I may be dumb, but I'm not stupid. Think about it. Besides, I left the room with you at break, don't you remember? We were talking about the student council election. Someone just wants to get me in trouble, and I'm going to find out who," I concluded.

"Yeah, you're right, PJ. I'm sorry I blamed you, but somebody in this class has a sick sense of humor and when I find out who it is, that person had better run for the hills. Heads will roll, you just wait!" Theresa blithered.

"I'm sure we'll flush out the culprit," quipped Mr. Cooper. "Right now we must press on with our history lesson. Everyone please take out your book and turn to page 218, the beginning of Chapter 11. Perhaps not by coincidence, we will begin our study of King Louis XIV of France. Hopefully we won't lose our heads."

Mr. Cooper surveyed the room to see if anyone had picked up on his humor. No one did, so he continued, "Does anyone recall how long the reign of Louis XIV lasted? No, well let's read and find out. Tanya, would you read first please?"

History is boring, especially when Mr. Cooper lectures. Most of us have learned to cope by drifting off into our own little fantasy worlds. We accomplish this feat with varying degrees of sophistication. Kristina was reading one of her romance novels which she had secretly concealed on her lap. Whenever Mr. Cooper turned away, Diana peered into her compact to see if any new pimples had appeared. Gus was fiddling with a straight pin. It looked as if he was trying to stick the pin into the eraser on his pencil. He's probably creating a new weapon of destruction to use on some unsuspecting victim later today, I thought. Billy, who is generally very shy around girls, is staring at Janelle on whom he has secretly had a crush since kindergarten. Of course Janelle knows about it and keeps poor Billy on a string. She uses him and he doesn't even know what's happening. I noticed that several other people besides myself were frantically trying to complete their math pages before we face Mr. Bakker next period.

Then a funny thing happened. God truly looked down from above and performed a miracle to save us from math class. Anyway, I reasoned that if God cares for the birds of the air like it says in Matthew and He answers prayer requests that come up repeatedly during our class prayer time for everyone's kitties and doggies, He most assuredly can intervene in our behalf for something as serious as math class with Mr. Bakker.

Mr. Cramer came into our room and announced, "A water main has broken. We have shut the water off to repair the leak. Unfortunately, it will take at least twenty-four hours to make the repairs. So, as much as I know it will break your hearts, Mr. Cooper will dismiss you by lunch time."

A chorus of "hurrahs" filled the room.

"Thank you, LORD!" I exclaimed, more loudly than I intended.

I better keep my mouth shut. The way my day is going, someone will probably blame the broken water main on me, I thought, as Mr. Cramer glared at me.

"Yes, PJ, God is so good. Now you have another day off and

right after winter break, too. I know some of you need transportation home. You may make your arrangements between now and lunch time. Mr. Cooper, please be sure each student takes one of these notes home," he said, handing a stack of papers to our teacher. "The note explains what happened and tells parents and guardians how to determine when to send the students back to school. If all goes as planned, school will commence on Wednesday."

"What about those of us who can't get a ride home?" asked Theresa, who carpools to school from almost forty miles away.

"Good question, Theresa. The nursery school will remain open for any students who need to remain for the day. The restrooms will be open. You just won't be able to flush," Mr. Cramer said with a straight face.

"Yuck!" squealed a volley of voices in unison.

When Mr. Cooper dismissed us, Gus and I were outta there, pedaling our bikes like fury to make the most of our freedom. Gus asked if he could come to my house until the regular time for school to be dismissed so he wouldn't be forced to spend the afternoon with the nursery school bunch. I was pedaling along without using my hands while gobbling down my sandwich and balancing a coke. Gus, riding his mountain bike behind me, was laboring to keep up.

We were directly in front of South High School, located within shouting distance of our school. It seemed as if hundreds of kids were suddenly catapulted from the doorways of the building. South High has an open campus which means students can leave the grounds to go to a fast food place or go home for lunch. Unfortunately, sometimes kids don't come back for their afternoon classes. I know, because I got the word from former students of John Mark who now attend South High. Just as I was riding (quite legally, I might add) across the entrance to the parking lot, a carload of kids came barreling toward me. I lost my balance and fell from my bike, skidding a few feet on my hands and knees.

"Watch where yer goin', jerk," someone yelled from the car.

I heard a string of profanity and then someone else said, "Use both hands while learning, kid."

Tires squealed as the driver accelerated and worked the black jeep through traffic to the far lane.

Gus jumped off his bike and rushed to my aid. I sat up slowly, brushed myself off, and looked down the street to catch a glimpse at the jeep as it turned the corner. Besides the tear in my new pants and scrapes on the palms of both hands, I wasn't badly hurt.

"Say, I saw the whole thing, and I got part of the license number. Couldn't catch it all 'cause my eyesight ain't what it used to be," volunteered an old-timer standing over me. "What I saw was 2FUR7, but they was gone too fast for me to see anymore. I walk this way often, and I can tell you for a fact, there's lots of accidents right here at this very spot."

"Thank you, sir," I said. Gus took my hand and pulled me up. I picked up my bike and checked it over carefully.

"You were lucky, dude. Those guys just about creamed you," commented a girl standing with a few other kids who had gathered about.

"That jeep belongs to Jared Whitney. His dad gave it to him for a Christmas present. If you need a witness, my name is Julie Stroud, and I'd be more than happy to fink on that creep. He's an accident waiting to happen."

"Thanks, but I'm okay, and he didn't hit me, so there's not much to tell," I concluded.

"Are you sure you're okay, PJ?" asked Gus.

"Yeah, I'm fine, but my mom's not going to be too happy when she sees these pants," I said as we continued riding toward my house.

"It's not your fault. There wasn't any way you could've avoided what happened," said Gus, trying to console me.

"I don't know about that. If my hands had been on the handlebars where they belong, maybe I wouldn't have lost my balance. God was watching over me, that's for sure."

The afternoon passed quickly. Needless to say, I didn't work on my math. Gus left at 3:00 o'clock, and I decided to spend the remainder of the afternoon working on the diagrams Mr. Cooper had assigned us. I didn't have in mind collecting the chocolate chip cookie reward, but English was one of my easier subjects and I figured I might as well get it out of the way. I finished four sentences, got stuck on #5, and all my good intentions went out the window. Finding my basketball in the garage, I went out front to the driveway to shoot a few hoops. Very quickly, I realized the fall I took did more than skin my knee. My leg was sore, and I felt a sharp pain when I drove in for a lay-up. I sat down on the grass to examine my injury more closely.

"Wow, what nice legs you have!" said Patti.

Little sisters! They can be such a pain.

Jezi was jumping up to lick my face. I pushed her away.

Mom, noticing the scrape and dried blood on my leg, said, "PJ, what happened to you?"

"It's nothing. I just fell off my bike coming home from school."

"Oh, quit being so brave," she said. "You can tell me all about it while I clean that nasty scrape. Looks like your pants are beyond repair."

But that's all she said. Mom patiently listened to my story about the guys who almost hit me, and I didn't get the lecture I expected about ruining my new pants.

"So many kids these days just don't think about consequences. Imagine having to live the rest of your life with the knowledge that you were responsible for the death of another person. You could've been killed, PJ. I know it wasn't luck. God was taking care of you because you belong to Him," she said.

Mom turned away quickly but not before I saw the tears in her eyes. "I'm going in the kitchen to see what I can rustle up for supper. Your dad will be home late because he has a meeting. Would you and Patti like to eat in the family room?" she asked.

"Sure, Mom, whatever," I answered.

Most of the time our family eats meals together. Lately, however, with Dad trying to get the computer business going, there have been several times when Mom either took us out for fast food or ordered a pizza. I kinda liked the arrangement because we could watch TV while eating, but I know it bothered Mom. She thinks mealtime is right up there with Sunday worship service. It's a time for sharing our day, sharing our plans, and all that stuff. Jezi likes eating in the family room best of all. I think she mentally calculates the food that will come her way if she plays her cards right. Tonight was no exception, but I think she took the menu a wee bit too personally.

When Mom brought out the hot dogs and sauerkraut, she immediately made two enemies. Personally, I love sauerkraut which is one reason why my mom makes it. Patti almost barfs at the sight of the stuff. Jezi is a perfect copycat. When Patti made a scene about the yucky sauerkraut, Jezi totally upstaged her. Mom placed Patti's tray on the floor beside her and turned to deliver mine. Jezi approached Patti's tray cautiously, sniffed the contents from a safe distance, walked backwards for a few feet, and then took off running around the room like a cat was after her. She ran behind the rocker, across the tile in front of the fireplace, leaped on the cushions on the couch, shot across the back of the couch banked like a race car at Laguna Seca, and was beginning the whole routine again when she accidentally cut the lap short and landed in Patti's lap. Unfortunately (or fortunately if your name happened to be Patti), Patti was holding her plate full of sauerkraut and wieners on her lap. I've never seen anything so funny in my life. Jezi and that sauerkraut became as one when the plate shot into the air and sauerkraut rained down upon both Patti and Jezi. When the sauerkraut had settled, Jezi sat there in the midst of it with a frankfurter between her teeth and a silly expression on her face. It was as if she were saying, "Ya, Mom, da vieners is fine but let's not have any more of dat kraut stuff."

While Patti and Mom were cleaning up the mess, I turned on the TV. The evening news was just beginning. The mangled remains of a vehicle which had come to rest meshed against a huge tree filled the screen. The commentator stated that this single-car accident had occurred at about 2:15 p.m. when the driver, a young girl only fifteen years of age, failed to negotiate a turn while driving at a high rate of speed. The reporter went on to state that several of the young people were thrown out of the convertible on impact with the tree. All five occupants of the vehicle were killed instantly.

Mom, who had stopped what she was doing, stood transfixed before the TV. Her face was ashen. "PJ, was that the car that almost hit you today?" she asked.

CHAPTER FIVE

WHAT'S A FRIEND FOR?

A friend sticks closer than a brother.
— Proverbs 18:24

My knees were shaking as I walked over to answer the phone which was ringing off the wall. With my eyes still glued to the TV, I picked up the receiver and stood there in a daze holding it to my ear.

"Hello . . . hello! Is anyone there?"

I recognized Gus's voice and responded, "Oh, yes, Gus. I'm sorry. Say, I'll call you back in a few minutes, okay?" I stammered.

"Are you watching the news?" he asked.

"Yes, I'll call you back soon," I said, hanging up the phone.

"Come over here and sit by me," my mom directed.

My mind was numb as I moved to join her on the couch. The news reporter concluded her remarks about the accident and began discussing another story.

"That was the same car, wasn't it, PJ?" questioned my mom.

"I'm pretty sure it was. The car in the accident was a black jeep with no top, but there were only four people in it. The reporter said they were students from South High who evidently decided to take the afternoon off. The thing that confuses me is that there were five guys in the car that almost ran over me, and I'm certain a boy was driving, not a girl," I said.

"Well, it's tragic whether it was the same car or not. They were awfully young," said Mom. "Just think of the agony the parents of those four kids are going through right now."

Before I went to sleep, I prayed for the families of those kids. Sleep was a long time in coming. This was the first major confrontation I had ever had with the issue of death. It's so final. I was taking the whole thing very personally even though I didn't know any of the kids who were killed. The thought passed through my mind that perhaps they would still be alive if I had called the police and reported them. Maybe the police would have gone after them with the partial license number the oldtimer had given me and a description of the jeep. I finally fell asleep by saying John 3:16 over and over.

The telephone rang as I was sitting at the table eating a bowl of Coco Pops the next morning.

"You didn't call me back, PJ. You said you'd call me back," responded an irritated Gus.

"Gee, I'm sorry, Gus. The news last night really shook me up. You were calling me about the accident, huh?" I asked.

"Well, yeah, sure. I mean, those were the guys who almost ran you down yesterday. "Have you seen the paper this morning? A picture of that jeep plastered against a tree and the news story about it take up most of the front page." Gus has a paper route, so he's up early and usually knows what's on the front page of the paper. Every Wednesday when we share current events in history, Gus has the newspaper and is prepared to share. He picks the goriest things he can find to share, too.

"Are the names of the kids given in the paper?" I asked.

"Yeah, and that girl with the wad of gum was right about the jeep. It belonged to Jared Whitney whose father had given it to him as a Christmas present, according to the paper. He just completed driver training last month, but the highway patrol is fairly certain he wasn't driving at the time of the accident. The officer says the girl was driving the jeep. Let's see, it's right here. Yes, the girl's name was Tiffany Moffett," Gus reported. "She was only fifteen years old and a freshman."

"Tiffany Moffett! Are you sure? Gus, don't you remember her? Tiffany went to John Mark a few years ago. She, Janelle, and Dawn were friends. Don't you remember? Tiffany always used to hang around with kids in our class. Does the paper say what caused the accident?" I asked.

"No. Of course it's under investigation, but the paper doesn't give any details about that or why they were out of school," said Gus. "They might've been drinking or on drugs. I'm going to look in my past yearbooks and see if I can find a picture of Tiffany Moffett. I don't remember her at all. Why don't you come over? We can go to the mall later."

"I don't know. I just want to get my mind off that accident," I said.

"What better way to do it, man?" I'll bet most of the girls in our class are at the mall since there's no school today. Come on, PJ. Let's go check out the babes."

"You sound like Kent, man. I'll be right over but not to check out the babes."

The first thing we checked out at the mall was the Arcade. In fact, we remained sequestered there with the video games until lunch time. Then we cruised from one end of the mall to the other but saw no one of consequence. Abandoning the search for babes, we decided to dine at the Burger King across the street. Low and behold, our search came to an abrupt end. The place was jumping. It was lunch time and kids from Washington Middle School had invaded the place like a horde of locusts. We stood in the long line waiting to place our order and listened to the banter occurring among the kids. Much of the language was gross and the kids were using lots of profanity, but other than that, they sounded a lot like us. One thing you do not hear on the campus at John Mark Christian School is profanity. The Bible says, "As a man thinks in his heart, so is he." I just praise God I haven't learned that language. The guys talked about chicks, and the girls talked about hunks. They talked about their teachers, too much school work, persons they hated, and food. Someone mentioned the accident which led to a discussion about death. The prevailing opinion among the group was that when a person dies, that's the end of it. There is no life, nothing to look forward to, after one dies. Naturally, this led one girl to expound her beliefs about reincarnation.

We missed the rest of the conversation as this group got their orders and headed for a booth. I noticed the booths around them were all taken, so I'll never know what she thought about reincarnation. Gus and I found a place and began feeding our faces.

"Psst, PJ, those girls are staring at you," whispered Gus.

"Not," I said, casually looking in their direction.

I heard someone at the table say, "I dare you," and the next thing I knew a girl about my height was leaning over towards me. She had blonde hair with long bangs in front, blue eyes, and the nicest smile I think I've ever seen. It was love at first sight.

"Pardon me, sir, but would you happen to have any Gray Poupon?" She was going to say something else but cracked up laughing, staggered backwards towards the booth, and sat down hard. She put her head down on the table, stomping her feet, and snorting like a pig.

Not to be outdone, after all I have a reputation to uphold, I casually took a match from its holder on the table, put the end of a french fry in my mouth like a cigarette, struck the match, and attempted to light the french fry. As I walked towards her table, I coughed as if the smoke from the french fry was choking me.

All four girls at the table had their eyes riveted on me.

"I have no Gray Poupon, my sweet, but my chauffeur says he has a cup of sugar in the limo you may borrow. Do stop by for a spot of tea," I said, brushing my hair back with the palm of my hand.

Now Gus was cracking up. I sat down and waited for the next scene. I didn't have to wait long. I knew I had finally met my match when the blonde walked over and slapped my face, saying, "Oui, monsieur, but you are being too forward, and I shall tell my lover."

She took off following the other three girls who were running out the side door.

Kids in the immediate area were staring wide-eyed during the whole scene. A roar of laughter and scattered applause filled the room. I stood up and took a bow. Gus headed for the door muttering, "I'm outta here, dude."

We retrieved our bikes and headed for my house.

"Well, how do we top that for entertainment?" I asked.

"Let's get your basketball and go shoot some hoops at school," Gus offered.

We were surprised to see several cars in the parking lot, and a bunch of junior high girls on the basketball court. Miss McPeek, a second grade teacher and the junior high girls' coach, was with them. Peggy and Amy, otherwise known as the "twin towers" because they are so tall, were at the drinking fountain. Two guys were shooting hoops at the far end of the playground. I couldn't make out who they were.

"You guys just can't stay away, huh?" asked Peggy.

"So, looks like we're in good company. Why are you here?" asked Gus.

"Well, we have a game tomorrow, so we've been practicing for the past two hours," said Amy.

"You need it," I said, again sticking my foot in my mouth.

"Hey, look who's talking. I'll have you know our team is great. We haven't lost a single game," said Peggy. "Would you care to tell us how your team is doing?"

How embarrassing! The boys team hasn't won a game. Only three out of the six guys in eighth grade are out for basketball, and the seventh graders haven't been much help because they are so short and inexperienced. Usually the boys have a winning season and the girls lose. In fact, this is the first year anyone can remember that our girls have done so well. They were so happy when they won their first game before Christmas that they were all crying. Girls! Who can understand them?

Miss McPeek called the girls, so Gus and I shot a few baskets and then played a game of one-on-one.

"Care if I join you?" asked Kent.

"Where'd you come from, man? Aren't you supposed to be in school?" asked Gus.

Kent smiled, twirling the basketball he was holding on one finger. "I'm sick, can't you tell? My brother called the office and gave them a phony excuse. Anyway, you guys have the day off, so it's only fair for me to take off and hang out with my old buds. Right?"

I should've kept on shooting and not said anything, but I guess that's just not my nature. Anyway, I blurted out, "Aren't you making things even worse for yourself, Kent?"

"Wha' da ya mean by that?" asked Kent.

I should have listened to the little voice in my head telling me to cool it.

"Aren't you already in trouble with the police?" I asked. There, I said it. I guess deep down I wanted to know the outcome of Kent's trip to the police station, but it quickly became apparent that he wasn't in a mood to share.

Gus, sensing a brawl about to happen, said, "Looks like the girls are done practicing. Let's go see if they will play a game with us." He took off leaving Kent and me facing each other.

"Come on. Make your move, PJ," Kent said angrily.

"Hey, I don't want to start anything. I'd just like to help, Kent. Don't you remember how we used to talk to each other when we had problems? What are friends for? I just want to be there for you if you need to talk."

He moved closer, almost in my face. "I don't need your friendship, man. You just keep your nose out of my business," he said. "Every time I hang around with you, something bad happens to me. It's like you're jinxed or something. I used to think you were my friend. You've changed, PJ. Maybe it's all that religion you have stuffed in your head, I don't know. Just keep your comments to yourself and leave me alone."

"Whatever," I said. "One of these days you'll need someone to talk to, Kent. If you keep pushing your friends away, you won't have anyone to turn to when you need help."

"Shove it, man. I'm sick of you," he said, as he turned and walked away.

I walked directly to my bike and was about to ride off when Gus jogged over to me.

"Where are you going, PJ?" he asked. "The girls said they'll take us on. We can't let them beat us. Come on, we need you."

"For the good of all concerned, I better go home. I still have math to do. If I stay, I'll end up getting into a fight with Kent."

"What is it with you and Kent anyway? You guys used to be such good friends."

"I'd like to tell you, but I can't. I just hope Kent gets some help before it's too late," I said. "I'll see you tomorrow."

CHAPTER SIX

IF I SHOULD DIE

I, even I, am he who blots out your transgressions, for my own sake, and remembers your sins no more,
— Isaiah 43:25

My relationship with Kent remained strained for the next few weeks. I stayed away from youth group knowing in my heart that avoidance wasn't the answer, but Kent seemed to feel I was somehow responsible for all of his problems, so my presence just agitated the situation. Kent and I have had our differences, but we always seemed to work them out. Now he seems to be loaded with problems of his own making. I mentally went through some of the problems I was aware of that Kent was facing. He was expelled last fall from John Mark for a myriad of things; the judge gave him a year's probation for the shoplifting thing; he ditches school; his language is totally offensive; and I know his situation at home isn't the greatest.

Things aren't all bad though. During the time I've stayed away from youth group my grades have improved. My parents were so pleased with my mid-quarter progress report, they gave me their blessings by paying my fee to attend winter camp. I was motivated to go because I knew Kent wouldn't be there. That's cruel, I guess, but I knew there wasn't room at that camp for the both of us. I need to talk to someone about Kent. It bothers me that he has mentioned suicide. I haven't spoken to a soul about that. Sometimes when problems mount up a person can feel overwhelmed, especially if that person isn't depending on God.

Student council elections were held before we went to camp. Everyone was totally surprised when Theresa was elected president over a popular seventh grader named Charlie. Janelle is the vice-president, Kristina is secretary, Peggy is treasurer, and I was chosen to be the spiritual-life leader. I don't feel worthy to hold such a position, but when I shared the news with Pastor Bob, he promised to help me. My main function is to open meetings with prayer and read a passage from the Bible.

Once again, I'm surrounded by women. There are a few male room representatives and Mr. Cooper, our advisor, but I'm the only guy serving as an officer. Our meetings are conducted in a very businesslike manner. Mr. Cooper lets the officers totally take charge.

Theresa adjourned our meeting early because the officers needed to discuss the final details for the leadership conference.

"Get a good night's sleep. Remember, we leave from the parking lot in the morning at 5:00 sharp," Mr. Cooper said.

"I don't see why we have to leave in the middle of the night," protested Janelle.

"Yeah, I'll have to get up at 4:00 so I can fix my hair," I joked.

Theresa let loose one of her infamous laughs which scared a couple of the fifth grade representatives and rattled the windows.

"You of all people shouldn't complain, PJ. I know you like to eat. If we don't leave at 5:00, we'll get stuck in commuter traffic and won't have time to stop for breakfast. Of course, I could bring some cookies," said Mr. Cooper.

"Cookies! Did someone say cookies? We'll eat the cookies," said one of the sixth grade representatives.

"You do not want these cookies, dearie," said Theresa.

"I'll be here, Mr. Cooper. I might come in my pjs without my hair combed, but I'll be here. Just please spare us the cookies," said Peggy, on her knees in a pleading position.

"Just make sure you use Scope and plenty of Right Guard. I

have a very sensitive nose. Since I'm the only boy, I get to ride shotgun. Right, Mr. C?" I asked.

"Sounds fair to me. I wouldn't want to turn you loose in the back of the van with a bunch of wild women," teased Mr. Cooper.

The bell rang to begin the day.

Bible is my favorite subject even though I keep it a secret and tell those who want to know that lunch is my favorite class. Once a week we have chapel with Pastor Bob — that's on Wednesdays. At least once a week we have a quiz or a test. There's always a passage to memorize related to what we are studying. Usually on Fridays Mr. Cooper conducts a question and answer session about things that are on our minds. Since the student council officers and Mr. Cooper will be gone on Friday, we had the discussion a day early.

"I hesitate to asked this question, but here goes," said Mr. Cooper, sitting on his tall stool as usual. "Okay, what's on your minds today?"

Mr. Cooper teaches sixth grade English before Bible, and some days they give him a rough time. His mood is usually obvious, but Maggie makes it a point to ask how his day is going anyway. Sometimes that even brings him out of a bad mood.

"Yes, Maggie, I see your hand," said Mr. Cooper. "And what intellectually stimulating question would you like to ask today? Nothing about the sixth graders, please."

"Aw, Mr. Cooper, that's not fair. I was just wondering why it smells so bad in here when the sixth graders leave?"

"Is that a theological question, Maggie, or are you really in the dark about it?" asked Mr. Cooper.

"Well, someone needs to tell them to use deodorant or something," said Maggie. "It really stinks in here when they leave."

"I'll convey your message, Maggie. Now, does anyone have a serious concern today?" asked Mr. Cooper.

"Yes, Sir, I have a question," said Lori.

"Let's hear it, Lori," said Mr. Cooper.

"Well, you know how you were talking about being forgiving the other day? I was just wondering what happens when a person dies and hasn't been forgiven for something? God told us to confess our sins, but if we die before we confess them, does that mean we won't go to heaven?" asked Lori.

Lori was fitting into our group nicely. She was the daughter of a Baptist minister, and we were beginning to respect what she had to say about the Bible. Several people were smiling as she finished her question.

"I just love to hear her talk that funny way," said Hunt.

"That's the way all people talk in God's country, Hunt. What do some of the rest of you think about Lori's question?" asked Mr. Cooper.

"It says in 1 John 1:9 that if we confess our sins, God will forgive us. Maybe God knew we were going to sin and forgives us in advance," I offered.

"I think that's pretty close, PJ," said Mr. Cooper. "How were the sins of people living in Old Testament times forgiven?"

"You told us people had to offer those bloody sacrifices all the time," said Gus.

"Blood sacrifices, Gus. That's correct. Each and every time they sinned, they had to offer a sacrifice. The process went on and on; it was never complete. Believers died and went to an intermediate place awaiting Christ's death on the cross. When Jesus Christ died on the cross, the sins of all humanity were placed on Him. He died for all our sins, past, present and future. So, if a person sins but then dies before he confesses, God has already forgiven him."

"Then why do we have to pray and asked Him to forgive us?" asked Diana.

"You need to keep in mind the reason why God created man. God created us to have fellowship with Him. He wants to have a personal relationship with us. Also, He knows that when we confess our sins, it conveys the attitude of our heart. God knows what we think, He knows the attitude of our heart, and He also knows we are finite, that we aren't perfect and make mistakes, and His forgiveness totally encompasses us the way we are."

"You know those four kids from South High who were killed in that wreck a few weeks ago? Tiffany was my friend. I think she was a Christian. At least she made a decision and was baptized. She was driving that jeep, and all she had was a learner's permit. They say the accident was her fault. How can God forgive her for that?" asked Diana. She wiped her eyes with a tissue.

"I think our concept of God is too small. God is all-powerful and all-knowing. There are big words to convey that, but the idea is that God forgives all sin. In our eyes a sin may be big or small, but God doesn't see them that way. If your friend was a Christian, Jesus paid for that sin when He died on the cross, and she is in God's presence right now just like the thief who died beside Jesus."

"Doesn't the Bible say somewhere that God doesn't remember our sins?" asked Lori.

"Yes, He removes them as far as the east is from the west. Someone use the concordance and see if you can find the reference," directed Mr. Cooper. "Good discussion. You guys are really asking some deep questions."

"I have a question, Mr. Cooper. What about a person who commits suicide? I heard that a person who does that can't go to heaven," I said.

"Mr. C, Mr. C," blurted out Hunter.

"Yes, Hunter, what is it?"

"I found that verse you asked about. It's Isaiah 43:25," said Hunter proudly.

"Good work, Hunter. Please read it for us."

"It says, I, even I, am he who blots out your transgressions, for my own sake, and remembers your sins no more,"[4] Hunter read.

"Back to PJ's question. Will a person who commits suicide go to heaven? I assume you are saying that the person is a Christian, is that correct?" asked Mr. Cooper.

"Yes, I think he is," I replied.

"So, it doesn't sound like this is a hypothetical case. First of all, PJ, if you know someone who is talking about taking his own life, you should take it seriously. People who talk about it often follow through, despite what research might tell you. If there is something you can do, you should try to get help for that person." Mr. Cooper paused for my reaction.

"Let's just say it's a hypothe . . . whatever you said," I cringed.

For once, everyone in the room was listening.

"Your question deserves an answer. I'm not an authority, and you should definitely talk it over with your parents — all of you, but this is what I believe. When a sinner believes on the Lord Jesus Christ and receives Him as his (or her) own personal Savior, he is born again. He has eternal life; he is a child of God. All Christians are sinners. We mustn't forget that. If we sin and do not confess our sin, our fellowship with our Father is broken until we do confess. If a Christian dies before confessing his sin, he is taken immediately into the Father's presence and lives with Him there throughout all eternity. There are two major things to consider. One, is the person a Christian? Only God can judge that. And two, the crux of the whole matter lies in the fact that Jesus paid for all our sins and that includes suicide. No one knows why a person commits suicide. It is unthinkable to me that such a thing could be done when one is in one's right mind. But whatever the reason, I know God is fair. Does that help or just muddy the water?"

"Yeah, thanks. It helps," I said.

"There's a little prayer we all learned as children, 'Now I lay me down to sleep, I pray the Lord my soul to keep, if I should die before I wake, I pray the Lord my soul to take.' In that simplistic little prayer, the one praying is acknowledging his security in God. When we believe and have fully trusted in God, we are secure."

Mr. Cooper hopped off his stool, and said, "Okay, it's almost time for lunch. Let's get with two or three people around you and share prayer needs. Each one in the group pray, and then I'll close by asking God to bless our lunch."

We came in from lunch all hypered up. Peggy, Amy, Janelle, Janie, and Sybil challenged us guys to a basketball game. We were arguing back and forth about the score. We won, but it wasn't anything to brag about.

"You guys don't play fair," shouted Sybil.

"Whoever told you life is fair?" I said, shrugging my shoulders and using Mr. Cooper's famous saying.

"That last basket shouldn't have counted," said Amy. "Gus

fouled me when he was going in for that shot. The ball should've turned over."

"Hey, hey, you guys, the bell has rung. It's time to settle down," said Mr. Cooper, raising his voice to be heard about the roar.

There was so much noise in the room, Mr. Cooper didn't hear the secretary's voice on the intercom.

"Mr. Cooper, the secretary wants you," announced Maggie, who was standing near the intercom.

"Oooh, Mr. C," said Hunter.

"You guys get quiet. Now!" he exclaimed. "Yes, Mrs. Nelson."

"Please send PJ to the office. He will be leaving for a dental appointment," she said.

"Are they going to pull all your teeth?" asked Maggie.

"That might improve your appearance," said Janine.

"Be nice to me. You keep it up and you'll damage my psyche," I announced, holding my head.

"Your what?" asked Gus. "I've known you all these years, and you never told me about no psyche. You're holding out on your old bud, PJ. I want one, too."

"You could use one, dude," said Janie.

I shoved my books into my backpack and was leaving the room when Mr. Cooper said, "PJ, would it be possible for you to leave the classroom in a less dramatic fashion? Work something out with the office, or whatever? Somehow I have the distinct feeling you girls are saying all these cutting things because the boys beat you at basketball. If that's the case, you need to save your energy and beat them next time. Right now I want you to get busy on your magazine assignment," said Mr. Cooper.

Sometimes I don't know if he is joking or being serious.

CHAPTER SEVEN

WHEN WILL I EVER LEARN?

My dear children, do not let anyone lead you astray.
— 1 John 3:7

Vacaville, the site of the leadership conference, is over 150 miles from our school. It was pitch dark when we pulled out of the school parking lot, and we drove and drove and drove. The girls occupying the back of the van were relatively sedate during the trip. The seven-passenger van gave the five of us plenty of room to spread out, so Theresa commandeered an entire seat for herself and slept the whole way. Janelle was quiet, which for her is very strange, but then her best friends Janie and Sybil weren't along to make her hyper. Peggy slurped on a jawbreaker, and she and Kristina incessantly talked about guys. They conversed using a strange gibberish which sounded like a mixture of pig Latin and pidgin English. Later, when it became light enough, they eyeballed all of the male drivers and rated their looks on a scale of one to ten, with ten being the highest. Whenever we approached or passed an eighteen-wheeler, they tried to get the driver to blow his air horn. Most of the time there was no response from drivers, but when the girls were successful, they went into all sorts of contortions and gyrations causing the van to sway slightly.

"Ladies, please, show a little respect. I can't sleep with all the racket and movement going on back there," said Mr. Cooper.

"Oh, Lord, help us all!" exclaimed Theresa.

"I thought you were asleep," said Kristina.

"Oh, say, Mr. Cooper, excuse me, but is there a restroom somewhere near by?" asked Peggy.

"Is that jawbreaker getting the best of you?" I asked. Peggy is perennially working on reducing an extra-large size jawbreaker down to nothing. The current one which she has been working on since January 3 remains the size of a half dollar.

"I'll stop at the next service station, Peggy. PJ, you should understand this scenario. If memory serves me right, you live in a household composed mostly of the feminine sex," responded Mr. Cooper.

"Yeah, I know. I forgot. When they gotta go, they gotta go," I said.

"It had better be soon, too, or else you'll have to pull over by some tall bushes," said Peggy. "You're lucky I'm not sick. I usually get car sick, you know. Sometimes I can't help it, and I barf all over the car before my dad can pull off the road.

"Oh, great, praise the Lord for small favors. I'm glad I'm sitting in the front," I moaned.

"Hang on, Peggy. There are some fast food places just ahead. We have plenty of time so we'll stop for breakfast, too. I'm two hours past due for my cup of coffee, and you girls need to arrange your faces, take your beauty pills, or whatever it is you do that makes you look so lovely," teased Mr. Cooper.

"I vote for Burger King," shouted Kristina.

"I love this place," I said, mimicking the guy in the TV commercial.

"We have a second to the motion. Any discussion? Sounds like it's unanimous. The motion is carried," stated Theresa, who was now in a seated position combing her hair.

While we ate, Mr. Cooper told us what to expect at the conference.

"There will be a lot of sessions to attend this morning. I'd like for each of you to choose a separate session so we will have more information to share. Take good notes. This afternoon will be fun. The host school has rented donkeys that play basketball, and . . . "

"Huh?" questioned Janelle, interrupting Mr. Cooper and coming to life for the first time.

"That's right, Janelle. The staff has challenged the student body leaders to a game of donkey basketball to make money for their mission projects this year. They purposely scheduled the event for today so other schools can see what a great money maker it is.

"How can stupid donkeys play basketball?" I asked.

"Easy. Players sit on the donkeys, pass the ball to each other as they work it down the court, and shoot. The donkeys are specially trained for it," said Mr. Cooper.

"How rad!" exclaimed Janelle.

"That sounds cool, man!" I added.

"That's not all, folks. The best is yet to come," beamed Mr. Cooper. "The game is fairly short, so we'll only be able to see the last part of it, but following the game the winning team gets to choose one person from the losing team to kiss a pig."

Just thinking about the possibilities with that kiss-a-pig stunt made the rest of the trip go quickly.

When we arrived, Mr. Cooper picked up our registration materials. We made our way to the church auditorium where the general meeting was held. The place was packed with kids just like us all dressed up in their Sunday best. Kristina and Peggy had put up a fierce argument to persuade Mr. Cooper to let them wear jeans. Of course they lost, and I'll bet they're glad they did now. Before the meeting began, they were spying out all the cute guys and making comments about them.

I admit I was eavesdropping, but hey, it just comes naturally for me.

"I think you guys should concentrate on our purpose for being here instead of flirting with the boys," I blurted out in my pious I'm-the-spiritual-leader voice.

Big mistake. BIG MISTAKE!

Kristina, sitting directly in front of me, turned around and gave me a look that would have crushed the Rock of Gibraltar. Except for the crowd, I do believe I escaped the second slap of my life by a mere split second. I knew that wasn't the end of it. I could just feel vengeance oozing from their brains.

"Why don't you get a life, PJ? Just butt out of our business, or you'll be extremely sorry," Peggy said angrily, struggling to keep her voice down.

Lucky for me, a lady with a guitar came to the platform at the front of the auditorium and began playing a familiar chorus. Kids began clapping their hands and singing along. I quickly got into the spirit and joined them.

After we sang a few more choruses, some guy who resembled Johnny Carson welcomed us, outlined the agenda for the day, explained that lunch would be on our own at fast food places, gave us directions to the various session rooms, and then sent us on our way.

"Okay, let's meet by the van following your last session, and we'll decide where to eat lunch," directed Mr. Cooper. "Remember to take good notes."

The session I attended was boor-ring. Some lady explained that the "real" speaker had had a family emergency. We were supposed to learn how to write a student body constitution. We ended up talking about politics the whole time. Maggie, a staunch Clinton fan, should've been there. She would've loved it. I must admit, those in the room who spoke up were well informed and did an admirable job of defending their positions, if you like that sort of thing. Personally, I was off in my own little world debating the advantages of eating at McDonalds rather than Taco Bell.

I steered clear of Peggy and Kristina during lunch. Or was it the other way around? We went to Taco Bell, ordered our food, and sat at two separate areas. Mr. Cooper, Theresa, and I grabbed a table near the front window. As if to drive home the point that they were still miffed at me and that I wasn't out of the woods yet because of my remarks, Peggy, Kristina, and Janelle ate at a table outside.

"How can you eat so much?" asked Theresa.

"Wha' da ya mean? This is only a snack," I mumbled with my

mouth full, and pointing with a taco in my hand to the five others in front of me.

I consumed those six tacos before Theresa ate one super taco and before Mr. Cooper finished two tacos.

"Mr. Cooper, do you give good advice?" asked Theresa.

"Well, I don't know. I guess it depends on the subject. What kind of advice are you seeking?"

She fidgeted for a moment and looked at me.

"I can take a hint. You want me to leave, right?" I asked.

"No, it's not really that. I don't care if you hear what I have to say, PJ," she said.

I could tell by the rather pained expression on her face that it would be appropriate for me to scat. "I think I'll go buy some more tacos. I've got this cavity that needs filling," I joked.

When I returned Mr. Cooper was saying, "Theresa, sometimes God doesn't answer our prayers as we want because He sees the whole picture. Some things we pray for aren't for our own good. It may sound silly to you, but sometimes I thank God for keeping me from all the harm that might have happened to me if my prayers had been answered as I wanted. God knows what's best for you and for your family. Just keep trusting in Him."

I could see tears in Theresa's eyes, so I took my tacos and walked outside where the other girls were. I felt like a man without a country. All the tables were full, so I had little choice.

"May I join you?" I asked. I didn't know what their response would be so I didn't sit down.

"It's a free country," said Janelle without looking up.

"Gee, listen, I'm sorry if I made you guys mad," I said, attempting to apologize to Peggy and Kristina.

Kristina put her arm around me and smiled sweetly, "We accept your apology, PJ."

I should've known better. I've known these girls for too long, and with all the time I've spent watching cartoons, I should've guessed they were up to something. I felt something cold slide down my back, and Kristina was rubbing it which made the ice even colder.

The whole thing happened so fast I didn't have time to react, and besides that my mouth was full of taco #9.

I got up and danced around pulling my shirttail out of my pants to let the ice fall free.

"Now, we're even, okay?" said Kristina.

Sounded like a good deal to me, so I said, "Sure, fine. We'll call it even."

Then I took a drink of my coke.

While I was dancing a jig, Peggy had emptied several packs of extra hot, hot sauce into my coke. I turned my head and spewed the concoction on the ground.

"I said WE, as in you and me, are even," laughed Kristina.

"Yeah, she wasn't speaking for me, but I guess we can call it even now, PJ," she said trying to put her arm around me.

"Oh no you don't. I'm not falling for the ice-down-the-shirt trick twice in one day," I said.

"Come on, PJ, I only want to give you a hug and ask for your forgiveness," said Peggy.

I was beginning to feel a little like Charlie Brown when Lucy always suckers him into holding the football, but I caved in reluctantly and let her hug me.

I assumed that was the end of it until Theresa stopped me as we were heading to the area where the donkey basketball game was being played.

"PJ, wait," yelled Theresa. "You've got something sticking to your shirt." She pulled the sticker off, read it, and almost created a scene with her laugh.

Peggy ran over and grabbed the sticker from Theresa, crumbled it up, and threw it into a garbage bin. She and Kristina then went over to Theresa and Peggy whispered something in her ear. They all laughed. People were staring at us.

"Okay, Theresa, what did it say?" I asked.

"Can't tell ya now. We got a game to watch."

I knew better than to push it. What had happened was my own fault for sticking my nose in their business. When will I ever learn? I'm outnumbered, and the girls badly outmaneuvered me.

If ladies did the maneuvering, I wonder if the word would be "outladyneuvered"? It had been a long day. I lined up on the blacktop beside Mr. Cooper, away from the girls, to watch the game.

CHAPTER EIGHT

SOME DAYS ARE LIKE THAT

If you make the Most High your dwelling, even the Lord who is my refuge, then no harm will befall you . . . .
— Psalm 91:9-10

What happened to the nice, quiet little group that was in the back this morning?" asked Mr. Cooper.

I could have made a comment, but quickly remembered the episode at Taco Bell and bit my tongue. I wasn't out of the woods yet, even though Peggy had performed the last provocative act by sticking some message on the back of my shirt. Theresa hasn't told me what it said yet.

The girls, all four of them, were having a grand time playing that rock-scissors-paper game. They laughed, sang choruses, and tumbled about, gently shaking the van with their antics.

Mr. Cooper and I talked about the conference some. He asked me about my family and told me a little about his. He seemed very proud of his four children, going into detail on the accomplishments of each one. The one he mostly talked about in class was his daughter who had completed a master's degree at age twenty-three. It was neat to hear him talk about his sons. One was good in sports and had been a Navy SEAL. The oldest was a musician. The youngest one, who had just completed a tour in the Army, was in college studying law enforcement. He hesitated momentarily, and then said, "That one scares me a bit. Since he was very young, he has been keenly interested in weapons. I wouldn't permit any of my children to even have BB guns when they were growing up. He has earned lots of awards and medals for marksmanship, and now he plans to spend the rest of his life in an occupation that's becoming increasingly more dangerous. He seems to be doing fine, and I know God is in control of his life."

As he was talking I remembered the battle I fought with my dad to convince him I was mature enough to handle a BB gun responsibly. Feeling rather guilty about my BB gun escapades, I changed the subject.

"Why did you become a teacher, Mr. C?" I asked.

He laughed, and asked, "That bad, huh?"

Oops, here I go again, I thought, putting my number nine's right in my mouth.

"No!" you're one of the best teachers I've had," I stammered. "I was just curious, that's all."

He told me more than I wanted to know, but it made the time go by more quickly and really helped me to understand him better. I could definitely see how he developed so much patience. My dad only has one son, and he has told me more than once that I'm a handful.

When we pulled into the parking lot at school, it was getting dark. Mr. Cooper opened the office so we could call our parents. Since it was the weekend, the girls had already made plans to spend the night at Peggy's. Before Peggy's mom came to pick them up, I asked Theresa one more time to tell me what Peggy had stuck on my back.

"I promised I wouldn't tell," she said.

"Just tell me this. Would I be mad if I knew?" I asked.

"Mmm, yeah, I guess so," she said. "But, PJ, I took it off, and nobody saw what it said but our little group. I'd just let it drop. Peggy and Kristina aren't mad any more."

"They shouldn't be after all the stuff they did," I said.

"See you Tuesday, PJ," she said, going to get in the car with Janelle, Peggy, and Kristina.

I had totally forgotten the presidential holiday coming up on Monday.

The way Tuesday began reminded me of the speech someone wrote about a terribly no good, very bad, downright awful day. When I discovered the classroom door still locked, I should've gotten a clue. While I'm usually the first student to arrive, Mr. Cooper is always the first teacher on campus. I stood around for a few minutes in the corridor getting wetter and wetter as the wind lashed the rain about, and finally decided to go to the nursery school to do some homework. I guess you've figured out by now that I avoid homework like the plague. I wait till the last minute and sometimes don't get it done at all. I usually do so well on tests that my average isn't too adversely affected. I checked once to see if Mr. Cooper had arrived, but he hadn't.

The bell rang to begin the day with a horde of us standing outside the room trying to keep warm and dry. A fine mist was still falling, but at least the wind wasn't blowing so hard. Mr. Cramer, the principal, walked jauntily along the corridor towards us. Mr. Cramer substitutes a lot when teachers are out, so I knew something was up.

"I'm going to be your teacher for awhile," he told us.

"How long is awhile?" Hunter mumbled.

Mr. Cramer doesn't miss a thing. "What's that, Hunter?"

"Oh, I just asked Gus if he saw that small child," said Hunter, pointing towards the office.

"Good, I wouldn't want to think you are unhappy with the fact that I'll be subbing," said Mr. Cramer, looking at Hunter sternly.

"We're glad you're here," Theresa said cheerfully.

"Five hundred points for Theresa," said Mr. Cramer.

When Mr. Cramer subs, most of us are on our very best behavior. No one would dare to do anything wrong. Actually, he is a neat teacher. He tells funny stories, and it's easy to get him off the subject. When he shares all of his boyhood stories with us, we don't have to work.

As we were taking our places and getting ready to begin I asked, "Where is Mr. Cooper today?"

"Mr. Cooper will be out for the remainder of the week. He called early this morning to inform me of his son's death," announced Mr. Cramer.

"Do you happen to know which son?" I asked.

"Yes, PJ, it was his youngest son who was working as a security guard when it happened. That's about all I know. Why don't we stop right now, bow our heads, and pray for the family," he said.

How could this be? I couldn't believe it. Mr. Cooper had shared his concerns about this son with me just three days ago.

After the prayer, Shiloh, probably the most sensitive and giving person I've ever known, asked, "Would it be all right if I got a card and passed it around for everyone to sign?"

"Sure, that's a fine idea, Shiloh. I know Mr. Cooper and his family would appreciate it. The school is sending flowers. Thank you for taking care of that," said Mr. Cramer.

It was my turn to lead the salute to the Bible in devotions, and I totally blew it. I had the Bible turned upside down and was holding it in the wrong hand. I had already said "attention, salute, pledge" when Mr. Cramer came over and stopped me. He didn't say a word, just took the Bible, turned it right-side-up, placed it in my left hand, and walked back to his former position. I felt like a real nerd. To make matters worse, Mr. Cramer thought I was joking around and let me know he didn't think what I had done was a bit funny. He didn't say it exactly in those words, if you know what I mean.

I got a zero in math for not having my homework finished, but I partially redeemed myself when I solved a difficult equation at the board which even Janelle couldn't get. I don't know what it is though. Whenever I do something really good, I don't know how to handle the praise. It's like I become another person or something. I get the big head and go totally wacko.

"PJ, if you don't stop making those weird noises, I'm going to send you out of the room," warned Mr. Bakker.

I stopped.

Ten minutes later.

"PJ, quit lifting the lid to that desk. You're distracting everyone around you, including me," said Mr. Bakker sternly.

I wasn't even aware that I was doing it.

Five minutes later I walked up to Mr. Bakker's desk and asked, "May I please go to the restroom?"

"You know my rule about that, PJ. You will owe me three minutes of your passing time if you leave during class time," responded Mr. Bakker.

"That's okay. It's an emergency," I said as I rapidly exited the room. When several kids snickered, Mr. Bakker said, "Please don't humor him. You'll just make it worse."

I heard his comment but kept walking. Sometimes I get the feeling Mr. Bakker doesn't like me very much.

Mr. Cramer made us line up like the fifth graders do to go to lunch. Then I discovered that I had forgotten to put my lunch into my backpack this morning. It was indeed turning out to be a terrible, no good, awful day. Now I would have no lunch. If we don't order a hot lunch when the count is taken first thing each morning, forget it. The cook makes you feel like you are stealing candy from a baby when you ask her if there will be any extra lunches. I decided to ask anyway.

After lunch, Mr. Bakker came over to talk to Mr. Cramer. When he left, Mr. Cramer asked Gus and me to meet him outside the door.

"Okay, it's time to confess, gentlemen," he said.

"Wha' da ya mean?" asked Gus.

I didn't say anything preferring to wait and see what the accusations would be. After all, I might be guilty.

"Mr. Bakker just informed me that you two were seen writing on the restroom wall. I've been trying to catch whoever has been writing on the walls for months," said Mr. Cramer.

"Mr. Cramer, we didn't do it. Gus and I were outside all during lunch. We didn't even go near the restroom," I said calmly.

"Is that true, Gus?"

"Yes, Sir," responded Gus. He was getting really nervous. Mr. Cramer had a way of helping you achieve that feeling whether you were guilty or not.

"Did the sixth grade boys say we did it?" I asked.

"Doesn't matter who said what. I just want the truth. Tell me the truth, and we can get on with our day," he demanded.

"I'm telling the truth, Sir. When I left math class to go to the restroom this morning, there was nothing written on the wall. I've been watching it myself and wondering who keeps messing it up after the custodian repaints it," I said.

"I want to believe you, PJ. Why do you think the sixth grade boys are claiming that you did it?" he asked.

"They just want to get us in trouble," blurted Gus, using the standard answer that has been overworked since the days of Moses.

"Well, keep your eyes open and see if you can help me catch whoever the culprits are. Let's go back to class and get some work done," he said.

And that wasn't the end of my troubles. I decided to go to youth group that evening even though we are having a major test in science tomorrow which I should study for. Gus said Pastor Bob was planning to take the group to a Giants game in the near future. I didn't want to miss that action, so I went to find out the details.

It's funny how you can try to avoid someone, and that's the very person you run smack into. Some days are like that. Kent was standing in the doorway to the fellowship hall where we meet, so there was no way I could avoid him. Pastor Bob once told us that Christians shouldn't worry because worry is a sin. It means we aren't trusting God. He said that most of our fears never materialize anyway. Trouble is "most" doesn't cover all the bases, and quite frankly, I was more than a little concerned about what Kent would do to me. We have fought before, but nothing serious. I'm not a muscle-man, but I can usually hold my own. Then again, I don't want to spend my life running from people or problems. I don't know what my reaction will be if he challenges me.

Lori was standing with Kent in the doorway. There appeared to be enough room for me to squeeze behind her without interrupting their conversation, which is what I attempted to do.

"Looks like they're fixin' to start," said Lori in her best southern accent.

"Too good to talk to us?" asked Kent sneering at me.

I turned and faced him. "No, I'm sorry, Kent. I just didn't want to interrupt your conversation," I said.

"Say, you'll, I'll see ya later. I need to visit the ladies' room before the meetin' begins," said Lori, sensing a storm approaching.

The noise from the music which is played before our program was almost deafening. Kent was almost yelling.

"Yeah, sure. Someone told me you've been staying away from youth group because of me. 'Fraid I'm going to beat you up, PJ?" he asked, coming towards me.

"Please don't start anything here, Kent. What I told you before still goes, I just want to be your friend. I don't want to fight with you. You think your problems will go away if you beat up on me?" I asked.

"It's worth a try," he said taking a step in my direction.

CHAPTER NINE

THE EYES HAVE IT

For God so loved the world that he gave his one and only Son, that whoever believes in him shall not perish but have eternal life.

— John 3:16

Pastor Bob really works hard to provide topnotch programs for us on Tuesday nights. He is an excellent preacher himself, but he also brings in youth pastors, Christian athletes, and musical groups to draw in more young people. It works, too. Tonight we are being entertained by a group called The Prisms. They play a soft form of contemporary rock music; in other words, it's very loud.

When Kent started towards me, I figured Armageddon had arrived. Kent has developed physically lots faster than I have. He pumps iron and is totally into bodybuilding stuff. I stood my ground, but my heart was pumping like crazy.

Fortunately, The Prisms made their appearance at that moment. The PA system in our fellowship hall is awesome. Each of the four persons in the group provided background music at his own microphone as the lead singer began belting out a popular chorus everyone knew. The sound emanating from the drums, electric guitar, singer, and over fifty junior high kids stomping their feet and clapping their hands was deafening.

As if baiting me and leaving me dangling on the line, Kent said, "It's not over, bud. I'll meet your outside later." Kent jogged right to the front of the group, clapping his hands and singing as if nothing had happened.

My knees were shaking as I walked over and stood beside Gus at the end of the row. Now I have to worry about what's going to happen. Why couldn't it just be over with, I thought.

I silently asked God to help me calm down.

Jed, the fellow who played the drums, had long hair and a beard. His physical appearance was quite out of place compared to the other guys in the group who were all clean-shaven with hair cut short. The lead singer was the spokesman for the group. When he introduced the others, he explained that Jed had just recently received Christ as his Savior and was the newest member of the band. Then Jed gave his testimony. Jed, who appeared to be about twenty years old, told us how his parents were both killed in a plane crash when he was in junior high. His parents were good Christians, but Jed had always rebelled against their religion. He told us how he blamed God for their deaths. He couldn't understand how a just and loving God could permit them to die. He hated God so much, he decided to dedicate his life to Satan. He dropped out of high school, became a member of a Satanic cult participating in all sorts of witchcraft, and made life miserable for anyone he knew who claimed to be a Christian. With all the bad things he had been involved in, he said up to that time he had never robbed stores, raped women, or killed anyone. But Satan takes you deeper and deeper into sin, so that before long nothing you do seems wrong. One thing led to another as he delved deeper and deeper into Satanic rituals. One time as part of a ritual, he participated in a ceremony by killing a baby that had been born to one of the girls in the group. The baby's blood was offered as a sacrifice to Satan. When he left the sacrificial service that night, he couldn't get to sleep. Lying on his bed he recalled how his parents had taken him to church from the time he was a baby. He attended Sunday school, sang in a children's choir, went to Christian camps, and was even baptized; but none of that meant a hill of beans. He rebelled against all of it and developed a reputation at church for being a troublemaker. His parents didn't know how to reach him. After many attempts at counseling failed, the children's minister actually told his parents to keep him away from Sunday school. His parents forced him to attend worship services with them, and he hated every minute of it. He recalled how he would tune-out the preacher and fantasize all sorts of vile things during the service.

Then Jed told us how he met God. While over at a friend's house, he heard a radical guy on the radio trying to make Satan worshippers angry enough to pick up the phone and call him. Well, Jed said he became so angry he wanted to reach through the phone and rip the guy's heart out. But that day God had a different plan for him. Jed said that as he was spewing out all the venom he possessed toward the voice on the other end of the line, God began working on him. He remembered how his parents loved him and tried to show him God's love. He remembered how Sunday school teachers and helpers tried to teach him about Jesus. He remembered the baby he had sacrificed. He remembered John 3:16. And he broke down. That day right over the telephone he became a born-again Christian.

There wasn't a dry eye in the place when Jed asked us to bow our heads and close our eyes. The group played an instrumental version of "Amazing Grace" that I had never heard before, but I'll remember it for the rest of my life. Jed asked any of us who felt life was too much to bear or that problems were too much for them to handle alone to come up and kneel down at the front for prayer. A stream of kids went forward, including Kent. I went home feeling that God had truly answered my prayers. He loves me, and He loves Kent.

Mr. Cramer had meetings to attend Wednesday, so Ms. Newman, the librarian. stayed with us until a regular substitute arrived. Let me tell you, there was nothing regular about this sub. I've had some bad substitutes in my day, but this substitute had to be the world's worst. First appearances certainly didn't win her any points with our group. She possessed all of the standard characteristics of an inexperienced substitute including nervousness, being disoriented and unorganized, and the thing that probably did her in was not being able to control us. I mean we totally went bananas. A photographer could have captured a classical picture of pandemonium in a junior high classroom at that moment as Peggy licked her jawbreaker, Diana peered into her compact, Theresa softly hummed "Nearer My God to Thee," Billy fired an airplane across the room, Hunter shot a basket from his seat to the trash can and shouted, "Yeah, three-pointer," Gus rocked back and forth in his squeaky chair, and Billy kept tapping Janelle on the shoulder until she finally got so mad she slapped him. This lady, who didn't know the difference between a noun and a verb, finally in exasperation sat down at the teacher's desk, put her head down, and mumbled, "I give up." Of course, our behavior was totally inappropriate, and I'm sure many of us will have tons of guilt feelings twenty years from now, but hey, we're in junior high so what can you expect? Fortunately, the period ended shortly after she arrived, and we wished her a good day as we exited the room on our way to science.

The sub's day evidently didn't get much better. When I went by the room on my way to the restroom, Kristen, a fifth grader, was sitting outside the door.

"What happened, Kristen?" I asked.

With tears in her eyes, Kristen said, "I got sent out here for saying 'pp'."

I laughed, but quickly gained control and asked, "What do you mean?"

She laughed, too. "When we are studying tenses of verbs, Mr. Cooper lets us use "p" for past and "pp" for past participle. All I did was asked the sub if I could use "p" and "pp". I guess when everyone laughed, she thought I was being funny, so she sent me out here. I don't know why she got so upset. Mr. Cooper even makes a joke about it."

"I know. I sure miss Mr. Cooper. I'll be glad when he gets back. See, ya later," I said, as I saw the sub beginning to walk towards the door.

When we came back for Bible class, one of the sixth grader's told me the sub had sent five boys to the office because no one would confess to taking a teacher's manual from her desk.

During creative writing Sandra was standing near the sub and noticed something strange about her eyes.

Sandra asked, "Why is one of your eyes blue and one brown?"

"Well, that's really none of your business, young lady, but for your information I'm wearing one blue contact lens right now. The other one was giving me a problem so I took it out," said the sub.

Lori, who plans to get contact lenses soon, asked a question about wearing them which launched the sub into a lengthy explanation about the whole process. Some of us were feeling a teeny bit guilty for our behavior, so we kind of mellowed out for the remainder of the day.

By Friday we were all ready for the weekend. Mr. Cramer, having learned of our antics with the sub, made frequent trips past our room to make sure things were going smoothly. We had mega-tests on Fridays and our minds were sufficiently occupied with reviewing and preparing so that we didn't have time to get into mischief, at least not in the morning. It started raining cats and dogs just before we were to go out for physical education so we had to remain in our classroom. It's really the pits when we miss PE. PE gives us an opportunity to vent all of our pent-up feelings and emotions. So, we had a "free" period. To call it a "study" time, as the sub suggested, would be a grave injustice to the word "study". If it had been any other day of the week besides Friday, we might have made it through the period without anything serious happening. I mean, no one was studying, not even Theresa and Lori.

Most of the girls were sitting around talking, and not very quietly either. The sub was at her desk checking papers, I think. A couple of days before, Stan had introduced a new weapon to us. It was a peashooter of sorts. A small balloon was attached and secured with string to an empty spool of thread. To use the weapon, you place a piece of unpopped popcorn into the opening, pull back on the balloon while holding onto the popcorn, aim, and fire at your target. There were four of these weapons in our room on that fateful day. We were randomly selecting targets in the room to attack. For some reason I looked at Lori, who was sitting three rows over from us and all the way in the back of the room. Lori appeared to be crying. She rubbed her eye and then put her head down on the desk. Theresa was saying something to her.

The bell rang to end the day, and I didn't think any more about it. Somehow we made it through another week. It wasn't pretty, but we made it.

I got up early on Saturday morning, put on my running shorts and shoes, and headed downstairs. In the kitchen I encountered a hyper Jezi. Jezi knows instantly when I'm going to jog. She never barks and gets hyper when I'm going to take out the garbage. She never wants to go to school with me when she sees me throw my backpack over my shoulder to leave. And she isn't even religious because she heads for the back yard and lays in the shade when we leave for church on Sundays.

"Take her with you, please, PJ," pleaded my mom.

"Ah, Mom, she just gets in the way. Her legs are so short she can't keep up with me," I argued, even though I knew it was a losing battle.

Jezi was now waiting patiently at the door as if she knew that her case was in good hands.

"Isn't she in heat, Mom? What if we meet other dogs?" I asked.

"How many times have you met other dogs at the lake this early on Saturday morning? She'll be fine, honey," she said. "Maybe it's time we let her have puppies anyway."

As I was attaching Jezi's leash to her collar, Mom said, "Don't forget, you have to practice with your dad for the puppet show tomorrow, and you need to get a haircut today. Your hair is a mess. Now let me hear the "p" word, PJ."

"I promise, Mom," I responded.

Actually, it isn't difficult to jog with Jezi. She is obedient, staying right by my side, and really helps me pace myself better then when I jog alone. Except for the situation before Christmas with the goose that saved her life, Jezi has never been a problem. Without a doubt, Jezi knows that particular goose, and barks a greeting whenever we are in the goose's area. But Jezi has learned her lesson and never chases any of the ducks or geese.

Things were going fine, and we were completing our third and final lap around the lake when Jezi suddenly pulled away from me. She knew exactly how to manipulate the leash in order to work her way out of it quickly and smoothly. I guess that just proves she only remains on the leash to please her master. Anyway, she took off running across the grass towards the lake. Deja vu, I thought. Here we go with the goose again. I should be so lucky. Then I saw the other dog. A small brown dachshund had spotted Jezi and was chasing her. As the dog got closer, Jezi began running in circles. Then both dogs disappeared from view as quickly as if they had boarded a jet for a honeymoon to Hawaii. Buff's owner, an elderly gentleman, and I stood dumbfounded.

In a short while Jezi reappeared alone. She trotted up to me, sat on her haunches panting heavily, and looked questioningly at me as if to say, "Excuse me, has anyone seen a brown, male doxie about my size?"

CHAPTER TEN

THIS IS SERIOUS STUFF

". . . Not by might, nor by power, but by my Spirit," says the Lord Almighty.

— Zechariah 4:6

Don't worry, young fella. Old Jefferson likes to chase 'em, but he ain't capable of doin' no harm, the old man said. "They would've made cute puppies though."

I wondered what he meant, but the answer became self-evident about that time as Jefferson came lumbering out of the bushes with his tongue hanging out and plopped down beside his master. Jezi made one more attempt to get his motor running, but conceded that it was a hopeless matter and came back to sit beside me.

Duh! How naive could I be?

We finished our lap around the lake and jogged home without further incident.

Saturday afternoon my dad and I practiced for the puppet show we were giving for the primary Sunday school children. We had been at it for over an hour when I heard my mom say, "He's in the garage, Kent. Just come on through all this mess and go on out there." She was in the kitchen preparing a Mexican dinner for us. She spares no messes preparing that meal.

I was surprised when Mom appeared rather than Kent.

"PJ, Kent would like to see you on the front porch," said my mom, wiping her clean hands on her apron.

"Why doesn't he come back here?" my dad asked.

"Evidently, he's quite upset, and it looks to me as if he has been in a fight or something. I didn't asked," she said, turning to go.

"Go ahead, son," said my dad. "We've got our act together pretty good any way."

Mr. Cooper would have corrected him for his misuse of the word "good", but hey, I'm no English teacher.

Kent was sitting on the top step staring off into space.

"Hi, dude! What's up?" I asked.

"I didn't know what to do, so I just came over here," said Kent, looking sadly at me.

I saw several cuts with dried blood on his face. He had a picture-perfect, classic black eye, and his top lip was swollen to twice its normal size.

"What happened to you?" I asked.

"My dumb brother beat me up. He thinks he's so tough. If I had a gun, I swear, I'd shoot him," said Kent. "He knocked down my door and threw me against the wall. He didn't give me a chance to explain or anything. He just started beating on me with his fists and kicking me when I was down. Man, my ribs feel like they're broken."

"Explain about what, Kent?"

"Aw, he says I stole some money from him. I swear, I didn't take his . . . money this time." He almost said a cuss word, but stopped before it came out.

"Did you tell your mom?" I asked.

"She wasn't home. She wouldn't have done anything to him if she was. She can't stop him. My mom can't control any of us. I guess I just needed someone to talk to, and you've been about the best friend I ever had, so I came here," he said.

"Let's go in the house and get your face cleaned up, Kent," I suggested.

"Nah, that's okay. I'll be all right. I don't want anyone to know about this, PJ," he said.

"We don't have to tell anyone. We can just go into the bathroom and put some water on it or something," I said.

"You guys okay out there?" asked my mom, peering through the screen door.

"Yeah, we're fine, Mom. Thanks," I said.

"Doesn't look fine to me. Kent, why don't you come in and let me give you some ice to put on that swollen lip?" she asked. "I don't want to interfere, and I promise not to ask any questions. Okay?"

"She means it, Kent. My mom won't tell a soul," I said.

Kent was on his feet, following her like a little puppy.

"Can you stay and have dinner with us, Kent?" asked Mom. "We'd love to have you."

"Well, I dunno. I suppose I could," he said. "I'm not going back to that house for awhile, that's for sure."

Mom kept her promise and didn't ask questions. Kent and I went to my room to talk. Kent talked. I mostly just listened.

"PJ, you know I went forward for prayer at youth group?" he said more like a question than a statement. "I'm so confused, man. I want you to know that I really wasn't mad at you. Yeah, I probably would've fought you that night, but I was just mad at the world in general. I've cussed at God so much that I know He won't forgive me. The other night I went into the bathroom and stared at an open bottle of aspirin. I actually poured some in my hand, and for the first time in my life I seriously thought about killing myself. I know that if I would've, I would burn in hell forever and ever. But, you know, if I don't do it, I'll stay on earth in a living hell for the rest of my life. Even if I don't kill myself, I'll probably burn in hell because of all the bad things I've done. I hate myself for all those bad things. I just feel like God has given up on me. What'll I do? I am so miserable and confused."

This was a Kent I didn't know. I was stunned. Kent was always so outgoing and popular. He was Mr. Macho, super jock, ladies' man, and always seemed to have everything totally under control. I really didn't know how to respond. I remembered Mr. Cooper saying that when someone talked about suicide you should see that they get help. How could I make Kent realize he needed help? I silently asked God to lead me to say the right things.

"I've known you for a long time, Kent. You're my best friend, and I hate to see you hurting like this. I'm no psychiatrist, and I know you don't need someone preaching at you. You gotta know that God loves you, man. He never gives up on anyone, and He's not going to send us to Hell for bad things we have done. You know that, don't you?" I asked.

"Yeah, I know it in my head, but it just seems like a bunch of words. It doesn't work for me. Some of the worst things in my life happen to me after meetings like that youth group the other night when I went forward and was feeling so good. I always promise God I'm going to do better. I try. I really try to be a good Christian, but God doesn't seem to help me," said Kent.

"It's not what we do, Kent. It's what God did for us when He sent His Son to die on the cross. Jesus died for all the bad things we could ever think of doing. We'll go to heaven if we believe in Him because of what He did for us, whether we are good or bad isn't the issue. I know, it sounds all preachy, but it's true, Kent."

"I guess God doesn't hate me, but I feel like He does sometimes. How can He love a loser like me?" Kent asked.

"You're not a loser, Kent. You've got lots of stuff going for you. I wish I had half your ability in sports, and the girls go "goo-goo" over you," I responded, trying to lighten up the situation a little.

"Yeah, but my grades stink. I got kicked out of the only school that could've done me some good. I can't help it. Sometimes I just want to say the hell (excuse me) with it and give up and kill myself. The way I'm going, I'll end up being a bum just like my old man is," he said.

"Pardon me, but it sounds like you need to stop feeling sorry for yourself. Try to trust God more, try harder in school, and stop all that negative thinking. Mr. Cooper says negative thinking is the root of most of our problems. We all have problems, Kent. Just look around you, and you'll find lots of people who have it tougher than you. Committing suicide is serious stuff, and it doesn't solve anything. I wish I could help you, Kent, but I don't know how. Say, would you talk to Mr. Cooper? I know he could help you," I said.

Right then I knew I had pushed too hard. Kent got up, threw the ice pack down, and started walking off.

"That's the guy who got me kicked out of school, and you want me to talk to him? He hates my guts. You've gotta be kidding, PJ. Tell your mom I'm sorry. I just can't stay for dinner," he said angrily.

"Aw, Kent, come on back. I didn't mean anything. I just feel frustrated because I want to help you and don't know how," I said, following him down the walk.

"I know you mean to be helpful, PJ. I appreciate it. A lot of what you said makes sense, and I'll think about it. I guess I just need to be alone for awhile. I'll see you later, okay?" he said.

He was gone, and I felt so badly. I walked back into the house and went in to eat a Mexican dinner I knew I wasn't going to enjoy.

My mom asked me about Kent at dinner. I shared some of the periphery stuff, but didn't mention suicide. I felt as if the load I was carrying was too great, but I didn't want to place my mom in a position of having to compromise on her promise to Kent. She promised him she wouldn't tell anyone about his problems. If I shared Kent's comments about suicide, she would go immediately to Pastor Bob with it. Besides all that, I didn't want to talk about such morbid things with Patti sitting beside me.

"Don't you think we should tell someone about the beating Kent got?" asked my mom.

"I suppose we could call Child Protective Services," said my dad, "but I'm not sure they could do anything."

"I know Kent would rather we didn't do anything at all," I volunteered.

"If something were to happen — say later tonight even — and we didn't report it, we would never be able to forgive ourselves," said my mom. Maybe we should at least notify Pastor Bob about the situation."

I cringed knowing that Kent would immediately put two and two together and figure out who finked on him.

"Could we just drop it?" I asked, showing my agitation.

"PJ, I feel we have to do something, honey.

I'll talk to Pastor Bob and let him know about the promise I made Kent. Pastor Bob should be able to handle it without revealing his source. With the bruises and cuts on Kent's face, Pastor Bob can easily open a discussion with Kent," said my mom.

"I guess you're right, but if Kent finds out, he'll never come to me for help again and our friendship will be totally down the drain," I said.

Jezi was content. She got more than her share of enchiladas from me during our conversation.

The puppet show my dad and I performed for the primary kids in Sunday school was the raddest one we've ever done. Dad writes most of the scripts we use, and all of them have a very clear Christian message. It's fun working with my dad, too, because he allows me to try different things. Like in this script, I use a high-pitched voice which totally brings the puppet to life. The kids did everything but give us a standing ovation. I'm quite sure they don't know what that is. Anyway, I was pleased with our performance. My dad says I could have a bright future with puppets. I do enjoy making people laugh, but I have my sights set on becoming a youth pastor. I suppose even a youth pastor could use puppets once in awhile, and Pastor Bob sure makes us laugh at times.

Sybil, Janelle, Joel, and I are working on a puppet show for the speech meet which will be coming up in May. As seventh graders we won a second-place plaque for an original puppet show we did. This year we are going for a first-place trophy.

There was an old-fashioned potluck in fellowship hall after the sermon, and I made up for any lack of appetite I had last night. The food was so good. I went back for seconds and thirds. Finally, my dad told me to cool it, or they'd have to take me to the car in a wheelbarrow.

When my head hit the pillow that evening, I prayed, "God, please help Kent to think clearly. Show me how I can help Kent to realize that he doesn't have to rely on his on strength; he can turn all his problems over to You. Most of all bless Pastor Bob and make the way clear so that he can talk to Kent without him knowing I told."

I fell asleep quickly but woke up in a cold sweat. In my dream I saw an extra large image of Kent hovering over me, saying, "Some friend you are! Now I'm dead, and you didn't care enough to get me some help."

I turned over and covered my head with the pillow, but it was quite awhile before I went back to sleep.

CHAPTER ELEVEN

GROUNDED

Do not be deceived: God cannot be mocked. A man reaps what he sows.

— Galatians 5:7

The words "Welcome Back, Mr. Cooper" were displayed on a large, colorful banner in front of the classroom. Kristina and Tanya colored in the letters on the banner I made on my new computer over the weekend. Each of us wrote a message and signed it. In addition, Shiloh purchased a really neat sympathy card which we all signed. Several kids in our room and lots of people in other grades brought in cards, some bought and some homemade. These cards along with a few flowers were on Mr. Cooper's desk when he walked into the classroom Monday morning. Of course, none of us were there because Mr. Cooper arrives at 6:30 a.m.

We had just come off of a very hectic week. Having three separate substitutes in a four-day period and maintaining your sanity is most difficult.

We really meant the words printed on the banner. Everyone of us was pleased to have Mr. Cooper back. Normally when he takes attendance and cafeteria count we are quite talkative. On his first day back, you could've heard a pin drop. No one said a word. Gus didn't make any funny sounds, Kristina wasn't sucking on her jawbreaker, Diana wasn't primping, and I didn't make my chair squeak. It was awesome, and I think it just about freaked Mr. Cooper out. The thing is, it stayed that way all the way through devotions and English class. Of course he thanked us profusely, but I guess we wanted more than that. We wanted him to tell us about his son's death, but he conducted business as usual until Bible class.

When we came into class for Bible, Mr. Cooper was sitting on his tall stool with his Bible open. Once again, we sat down quietly without performing our usual junior high antics. I'm telling you, that is most unusual for this class.

"I know many of you are wondering about my son's death," he said. "This is going to be very hard for me, but I'll try to share some of it with you if I can do it without breaking down. Death is so final. I know our son is with God right now, but it's so painful to lose someone you love. How many of you have lost someone in your family?"

Several hands went up.

It was evident that Mr. Cooper was struggling.

"Then you know how painful it can be. Danny was our youngest son. He was twenty-two years old. At his funeral I asked the pastor to share two passages of Scripture, John 3:16-17 and Isaiah 40:28-31."

Mr. Cooper read the passage from Isaiah. He made it through the last verse and asked us to bow our heads. Tears were rolling down his cheeks. For a few moments there was absolute silence. Then Mr. Cooper prayed. While he prayed, I prayed too. I asked God to help him with the pain and grief he was feeling and to help him know his son was safe in heaven.

We wanted to hear more, but that's all there was. Mr. Cooper didn't even share with us about how his son died. Several girls were crying.

"I really appreciate your prayers. Keep praying for my family. I'm sure I'll be sharing more about this experience as the year goes on," Mr. Cooper said, tucking his handkerchief back into his back pocket. "I thought I could do it now, but I can't. I'm sorry. Let's get back to Matthew 5, the Sermon on the Mount. Someone tell me which verse you left off with last week."

Bible class was interrupted when the secretary's voice came on the intercom, "Mr. Cooper?"

"Yes."

"Please send PJ to the office now."

"Yeah! Busted!" sang out a cadre of people.

"I'm not going down easy. I'll take all of yooz with me, ya hear," I threatened mimicking a "Humphrey Bogart" voice as I walked out of the room.

I had expected Mr. Cramer to call all of those involved in the peashooter incident last Friday to his office first thing, and my anxiety level had risen steadily in anticipation. As I walked slowly to the office, I wondered why he only called me to the office. I already suspected that something serious was happening when Lori didn't show up for school.

"Go on in, PJ. You don't even need to take a number. Mr. Cramer is waiting for you," the secretary said, flashing me a huge smile.

Despite her friendly smile and my frequent visits to the office, I don't take these matters lightly. Believe me, a trip to Mr. Cramer's office is no picnic.

"PJ, we're looking at something very serious here. A young lady almost lost the use of her eye for the rest of her life because of one of these things," said Mr. Cramer, holding up one of the peashooters he had taken from the top of his desk.

I didn't say a word.

"What can you tell me about it?" asked Mr. Cramer.

"Did Lori say I did it, Sir" I asked.

"Lori doesn't know who did it. The substitute didn't know who did it, but she remembered seeing you holding one of these weapons. PJ, we've talked about this before — many times. Remember? If you are around trouble, you are going to be blamed. Your reputation is on the line when you do something stupid like this."

"But I didn't shoot at anyone, Mr. Cramer," I stated emphatically.

"Doesn't matter. I remember one conversation we had when I reminded you of what Paul said in 1 Thessalonians 5:22 about avoiding all kinds of evil. Do you remember? It wasn't that long ago. If someone goes into a store to rob it and you are with that person, the police will arrest both of you. Tell me who was involved? Who has these things besides you?"

"I gave the one I had to the substitute on Friday. Actually it wasn't mine. Stan made it. In fact, I think he made all of them. He was using one on the playground last week, and some of the guys asked him to make one for them. It just kind of spread. We were all using them, but only outside until Friday," I volunteered.

"Okay, who else has them besides Stan? Is Stan the one who shot the popcorn kernel at Lori?" asked Mr. Cramer.

"I'm not sure, Sir. Is Lori all right?" I asked.

"We'll talk about that later," he answered curtly. "Just tell me who else was involved on Friday, and I'll let you go for now."

I knew it would come out anyway, so I told him that Stan, Gus, Billy, and I were the only ones I knew who had the peashooters. Mr. Cramer let me return to the classroom after reminding me not to share our conversation with anyone.

Stan, Billy, and Gus were each called to the office, and then all four of us ended up there together. Stan had admitted that he made the peashooters in his garage and brought them to school. He turned over a couple of them he still had in his pocket to Mr. Cramer. What a dummy! You would think he would have sense enough to leave them home after Friday. There were now six of them on Mr. Cramer's desk.

"Gentlemen, I want you to realize how serious this is. I do not ever want an incident of this nature to happen again. Do you understand me?"

"Yes, Sir," we all responded in unison.

"Billy admitted that he was the one who shot the popcorn which hit Lori, but you were all involved. It could have been any one of you. Therefore, I'm going to suspend all of you," said Mr. Cramer, tapping one of the peashooters on his desk for emphasis.

"I'm dead," sighed Gus.

Billy actually started bawling, and begged Mr. Cramer not to tell his parents.

Stan didn't react at all.

And I just waited to see what was coming next.

"Stan, you brought the blooming things to school, so your suspension is for the remainder of the week. Billy, what you did was a very careless act. You could have permanently damaged Lori's eye. Then you lied to me about it. You were very wise in finally owning up to it. I'm suspending you for two days. Gus and PJ, I'm calling your parents and sending you home for the remainder of the day and all day tomorrow. Your parents will all need to check you back into school by having a conference with me," Mr. Cramer said. "Oh, and one more thing. I want each of you to write an apology to Lori, deliver it to her personally when you return, and let me know that you did so. Is that clear?"

We nodded our heads.

My parents were upset at me, and they totally took Mr. Cramer's side. I didn't really think the punishment was fair and tried to argue the point with my dad. Big mistake. In addition to the suspension, my dad grounded me for a week. That meant no TV, no friends over, no youth group, no nothing! I wasn't totally cut off from the world though. Either by oversight or as an act of leniency they forgot to take telephone privileges away. Whatever the reason, I took full advantage of it. I called Stan, but his mom informed me that he couldn't come to the phone. Then I called Gus and we rapped about what happened. His punishment was similar to mine. After dinner, Janelle called me, and I related the sad facts about all of our suspensions. Of course, she had already heard most of it. The girls in our room have a communication network they could probably sell for a good price to a third-world country. I hung up the phone and had taken only two steps when the phone rang again. This time it was Sybil. I talked to Sybil for awhile and then went back to my room. I heard the phone ring again and ran to answer it. My dad headed me off at the pass. He answered the phone, and told whoever it was that I wouldn't be taking any more calls. All the while he was looking at me with his professional-dad-type look. He didn't need to further verbalize his message to me. I realized there would be no further communication with the outside world until I returned to school on Wednesday.

I filled up half a trash can trying to write out an apology to Lori.

Everything I wrote sounded really corny. Then in frustration, I dug through the trash and found one of my first attempts, recopied it, and stuck it into an envelope with her name on it.

Tuesday was the longest day of my life. My dad took me with him to the computer store where I had to unpack boxes, dust shelves, clean the storeroom, and do a zillion other things. I was dead tired when we went to school to meet with Mr. Cramer that afternoon. He and my dad did most of the talking. I just sat there like a zombie and listened until Mr. Cramer asked me if I had learned my lesson. Of course I answered in the affirmative, and he told my dad I could return to class on Wednesday. I ate dinner, took a shower, and crashed.

Everyone let me know right away how quiet the classroom was without me. That made me feel great. I handed Lori the note I had written before class began.

"I'm sorry for what we did to you, Lori," I said in my most apologetic voice.

She looked around shyly to see if anyone was watching, took the note, and said, "That's okay. It really wasn't that big a deal. That was the first day I wore my contact lenses, and my parents got all upset. I'm so sorry you got suspended."

"It served me right. I got what I deserved. Like the Bible says, you reap what you sow,"' I said.

"But you weren't the one who hit me, PJ," said Lori.

"Yeah, but I was shooting at girls' on the playground. We were all doing it. I was just lucky I didn't get caught," I said.

Janelle came running up to us.

"Did you hear what happened to Stan?" she asked.

"Gladies and lents," barked Mr. Cooper. "It is time to be in your seats and ready for another exciting day here at JMCS. Why, it's better than your average soap opera, I assure you."

I really wanted to know what Janelle had to say about Stan so I hesitated even when he glared at me.

“Excuse me, Mr. Nichols. What is it about ‘go sit down’ that you don’t understand?” he asked.

I obediently went to my seat.

CHAPTER TWELVE

KATCH ME IF YOU CAN

For troubles without number surround me; my sins have overtaken me, and I cannot see. They are more than the hairs of my head, and my heart fails within me.
— Psalm 40:12

I was tempted to write a note to Janelle to inquire about Stan, but my intuitions told me to cool it. During passing time Janelle and Sybil accosted me before I even got out of the room.

"Do you know what happened to Stan?" asked Janelle.

"Yeah, I know already," I said. "He was suspended like the rest of us, just for a few more days is all. So what's the big deal?"

"You really don't know!" exclaimed Sybil.

I had to agree to that since my dad grounded me, and my communications with the outside world had been severed.

"PJ, Stan isn't coming back to school here. His parents have already enrolled him at Washington Junior High," said Janelle. "In fact, he starts there today. His parents had a really big argument with Mr. Cramer. They blamed the school for not having good teachers and are even threatening to sue."

"What!" I exclaimed. "You've gotta be kidding. Stan dug his own grave just as Gus, Billy and I did. His parents should know that. How can it be the teachers' fault when Stan was the one causing the trouble?"

We were going into Mr. Bakker's class, and he expects no talking from the moment we enter, so our conversation came to an abrupt halt.

Another one bites the dust, I thought. Last semester it was Kent and Dawn and now Stan. If we keep this up, there won't be a graduating class.

Math was boring. Mr. Bakker worked problem after problem, stopping only occasionally to ask if we had any questions. Most of us didn't understand his explanations, but no one would admit it. We learned long ago to keep our questions to ourselves and ask the smarter math students in our class — like Janelle, Shiloh, and Peggy — to explain what he was talking about later. That's a major difference between Mr. Cooper and Mr. Bakker. When Mr. Cooper asks us if we have any questions, he knows we do. He can tell by our facial expressions when we don't understand. Then he explains the concept in simpler terms or breaks it down so all of us get it.

As I'm so prone to do while he is talking, I let my mind wander to other, more important things. Boy, would I like to catch the person who is messing up the restroom wall. I noticed that the lame artist had struck again while I was on suspension. If Mr. Cramer observed the peace sign displayed in the restroom accompanied by the fact that I was absent from school, he should've concluded that I could not be the guilty party. Elementary, my dear Watson. You don't have to be a Perry Mason to figure that one out.

"Excuse me, Mr. Nichols, do I need to make an appointment to gain your attention?" barked Mr. Bakker.

Everyone was laughing when I returned to realityland. I heard Theresa's laugh above all the others, so I stuck my tongue out at her when Mr. Bakker was facing the board.

Mr. Bakker was being funny. Being funny at other people's expense is his way of gaining laughs. I really hate it when teachers use sarcasm. If Mr. Bakker only knew how much it hurts someone inside when he makes cutting remarks, maybe he would stop doing it. I figured there wasn't much I could do to change him, so I just blew it off. The class gets down on me when I don't actively provide entertainment during math and science periods. Quite frankly, some days I need to be entertained. Besides, I need to cool it for awhile if I want to remain on the student council. I'll be on probation now because of the suspension. If I blow it one more time, Mr. Cramer will see that my tenure on the Council is ended. I resolved right then and there not to be suckered into any more situations that even looked like they might lead to trouble.

It's funny how things work. Mornings go by so quickly, and we rarely get into any serious trouble before lunch break. After lunch it's like we're a different breed. I was walking behind Janie and Sybil as we were returning to class after the bell rang. These two young ladies who have been best friends forever were involved in a heated argument about something. I hurriedly caught up, stopping just a yard behind them, so I could pick up what they were saying.

"That's the last time I ever tell you anything," said Sybil.

"I didn't tell him what you said, I swear on the Bible. He asked me, but I promised you I wouldn't tell a soul and I didn't," stated Janie.

"Yeah, well everyone knows, so how did it get spread around?" asked Sybil, facing Janie with her hands on her hips. At that moment she saw me and said, "Butt out, PJ. This is none of your business."

Foiled again. Now I'll probably never know what or whom they were arguing about. During Chapel this morning Pastor Bob talked to us about harboring bitter feelings toward someone and not forgiving them. He said that even if the other person is absolutely wrong and we are one hundred percent correct, we should take the initiative and go to the person and ask for forgiveness. I hope Sybil and Janie listened and get their argument settled before our field trip on Friday. The seventh and eighth grade classes are going to Monterey to visit the Aquarium and the tide pools. Most of us have been there so often we are on a first-name basis with the fish, but the trip will provide a welcome diversion from class.

Mr. Cooper asked us to take out our creative writing folders and go to work on the magazine we are writing. We each have to complete a mini-autobiography to include on a page we are to design with all the good stuff about ourselves. I think I can fit my comments on a postage stamp. The assignment isn't due until two weeks before we graduate, so I haven't been too motivated yet. There are also weekly assignments like writing limericks about ourselves, drawing cartoons with clever punch lines, and writing "sick" junior high jokes and riddles. The good part is that we can work with a partner on the weekly assignments, so Gus and I have been working together. Only the best of the best will be printed in the magazine. Shiloh and Maggie are co-editors with Mr. Cooper having the final word about what does or doesn't get printed, of course. A quiet hum permeated the room as we mixed business with pleasure by conversing a little about our projects and a lot about our plans for the weekend or whatever else might be on our minds. Gus really dropped a bombshell on me.

"Have you seen Kent lately?" asked Gus.

"Oh, not for a week or so. Why, what's he up to now?" I inquired.

"He and another guy at Washington were fighting right in the classroom. They were going at it, man. You know how strong Kent is? Well, he totally went out of control. The other guy was getting in some good licks, so Kent went berserk and pushed him over a desk. Then he picked up the desk and threw it down on the dude. The paramedics were called, and they had to remove the guy on a stretcher. He was totally unconscious. I'm telling you, it was awesome the way Kent described it."

"So what happened to Kent, and how do you know so much any way?" I asked.

"Kent told me all about it yesterday when I saw him at the mall."

"I thought you were grounded," I said.

"Yeah, yeah, but I sneaked out. My parents never knew I was gone. Anyway, if you'll quit interrupting, I'll finish my story," Gus said, getting a bit agitated.

"Okay, granny, but try to finish in this century," I joked.

"Kent was escorted out of the room and told to stand in the

hallway until the vice-principal came. Some guys told him the police were coming because he knocked the dude out, so Kent took off running. He first thought the worst that could happen would be a suspension, but when he heard the police were on the way, he panicked. Did you know he was already on probation?" asked Gus.

"Sure, but how'd you find out?" I asked. "He gets really touchy when that subject comes up."

"He told me he was caught shoplifting. Had to go before a judge and everything. If you ask me, his life is getting more messed up all the time," said Gus.

I didn't want to reveal what Kent had shared with me, so I tried to ease out of the situation. "Kent certainly hasn't made matters any better by running away. Running away from problems only makes them worse.

"I gotta stay out of trouble. My parents will ship me to Alaska if I get into any more trouble," said Gus.

"I relate to that. Say, let's try to get on the same team when we go to the Aquarium, okay?" I asked.

"Oh, sure, but we gotta get on a team with some cute girls, too," Gus said, bobbing up and down in his chair excitedly.

"Hey, cool it. Mr. C is looking our way," I warned. "Don't you think this is a good cartoon?" I asked, holding up my drawing of a tank being attacked by a helicopter for Gus to see.

"I don't want any cartoons full of violence and mayhem, PJ. You know what I mean, too!" exclaimed Mr. Cooper.

"But my cartoon makes a political statement, Mr. Cooper. Sure, there's a little violence in it, but that's the way the world is," I stated.

"Let me guess. You have probably drawn soldiers from opposing armies blowing each other up with automatic weapons and grenades. If that or anything like it is the case, you might as well deposit it in the trash basket. I won't even give you credit for something like that. Your assignment sheet sets out the guidelines, PJ. Please follow it, and let's make this a great magazine — one you can look at twenty-five years from now with fond memories."

"Back to the drawing board. I wonder if Charles Schulz had

this much trouble when he started drawing cartoons?" I asked, loudly enough for Mr. Cooper to hear me.

"Study Charles Schulz's cartoons, PJ. The experience will be a real eye-opener for you," said Mr. Cooper.

I decided to make a trip to the restroom to check out the art on the wall. I entered the restroom very quietly just in case the culprit was at work. No such luck, but sure enough, there was a new piece of work printed with pencil in tiny letters which declared, "KATCH ME IF YOU CAN." The message was followed by a peace sign encapsulated within a circle. I noticed that the message was written about three feet up from the floor which would indicate that the job might have been done by a short person or one who got down on his knees to compose it. The toilet flushed in the stall farthest from me. I quietly walked to the urinal and pretended to be doing my business. Dirk, a seventh grader, walked out of the stall zipping up his corduroy pants and talking to himself. He said, "And if he thinks I'm going to pay him for that piece of junk . . . " Then he saw me, and his face turned beet red.

I turned to face him. From the look on his face, I'd say I really surprised him. "Hi, Dirk, how's it going?" I asked.

"Oh, uh, just fine. I have to get back to class. See ya," he said as he hurried by me still fiddling with his zipper.

"Dirk," I called. "Wait a minute."

"Wha' do ya want?" he asked.

"I just wondered if you have a pencil I could borrow for a second."

"Nah, I don't normally bring my pencil to the restroom," he said sarcastically.

"Thanks anyway," I said.

Well, I guess I can rule Dirk out. That is, if he's telling the truth. I doubled back to the restroom to check the stall Dirk had occupied. I was almost overpowered by the stench, so I quickly checked the walls, saw no writing there, and started walking toward the door. Then I happened to glance at the paper towel dispenser. Stuck behind it was a tiny yellow pencil no more than three inches long. It was wedged firmly in place with only the very tip sticking out. First, I tried jiggling the dispenser, but it was solidly affixed to the wall. Then when I wiggled the pencil back and forth, the point broke. I stood there trying to think of what to do next when the restroom door opened and in walked Mr. Cramer.

"Well, well, what have we here?" he asked.

"I can explain, Mr. Cramer."

"Yes, I'll bet you can, and I'm going to give you every opportunity to do just that. Follow me, please."

CHAPTER THIRTEEN

TO THE RESCUE

As a dog returns to its vomit, so a fool returns to his folly.

— Proverbs 26:11

I accompanied Mr. Cramer to his office, which was beginning to feel like a second home to me.

"Innocent until proven guilty. That's the good old American way, right?" asked Mr. Cramer.

"Right, Sir," I responded.

"Well, I'm just dying to hear your story, so let's have it," he said. I secretly wondered if he was angry or amused.

Mr. Cramer didn't interrupt me once. His face remained expressionless as he listened attentively to every word I said. When I finished, he said, "Okay, PJ, you may go back to class."

I gave him a startled look but didn't bother to ask questions. "Thank you, Sir," I said, as I quickly made my way out of the room.

I had a feeling he didn't believe me, but I wasn't about to question my good fortune. Something was up. I decided that Mr. Cramer was definitely holding out on me. Glancing at my watch, I realized I had not only missed the rest of creative writing but also PE. In fact, everyone was exiting the room when I arrived. Gus stopped me in the corridor.

"Where have you been?" he asked.

"It's a long story, dude. I'll tell you later," he said.

"Well, you better talk to Mr. Cooper. He gave us a handout explaining things about the field trip tomorrow," said Gus.

"Okay. Thanks, Gus. See you tomorrow," I said.

"So, PJ, what's going on with you?" asked Mr. Cooper in his usual friendly way. "We missed you this afternoon — this whole afternoon."

"I'm sorry. I know no one believes me, but I was really trying to catch the person who has been writing on the restroom wall. I thought I had him, but then I ended up being had myself when Mr. Cramer came into the restroom while I was there. Now, I'm sure he believes I'm the guilty one," I said.

Mr. Cooper handed me a sheet of paper and said, "Sometimes it's best to heed the advice Solomon gives us in Proverbs when he says, 'As a dog returns to its vomit, so a fool repeats his folly.' Whoever is playing the role of the fool will be caught eventually, PJ. God's in control of every situation. He's even in control of the person who's vandalizing the restroom. Leave it in His hands. This paper tells you everything you need to know for the field trip. Your dad is driving, so you will be riding with all the boys in your dad's van."

I shoved all my books into my backpack, cramming the paper Mr. Cooper gave me on top, and shuffled out the door. It seems like the more I try to do what's right, the more I get into trouble. Sometimes I wish God would speak to us like He did to the people in Bible times. As I rode my bike toward home, my imagination drew me back almost four thousand years. I daydreamed about being with Moses on top of Mount Sinai when he received the Ten Commandments from God. Of course, Moses didn't know I was there.

"Who is the young man you have brought to my mountain?" asked God.

"Young man? Why, I have brought no one with me, LORD?" replied Moses, looking around bewilderedly.

"Oh, but you have. Look yonder in that cave," said the LORD.

When Moses left camp to talk to God, I followed him at a safe enough distance so that he wouldn't see me. I had sneaked into the cave when Moses wasn't looking. The cave was dark, damp, and musty. I felt like I was up to my ankles in goop, but I was on a mission and wasn't about to be deterred.

"Who's in there?" called out Moses. "Come forth at once and tell me why I shouldn't put you to death."

I quickly scooped up a handful of the mud I was standing in and walked out to face Moses. My knees were shaking.

"Look, Moses, you can use this clay to make tablets. Why, I'll even be your scribe and copy down the things God tells you. How 'bout it, dude?" I asked, striding up to him as confidently as I could.

Then I was jolted back to reality. I thought Moses was screaming at me but suddenly realized it was an old man in the crosswalk whom I had almost hit. Now I'll never know the outcome of my daydream.

"You watch your step, sonny! Ya almost knocked me on my kazoo. Better pay attention or you'll end up in an accident," he said, waving at me frantically with his walking cane.

"Sorry, dude," I said, but I continued riding and didn't even slow down.

I was miffed because the old man spoiled my fantasy, but then Moses was probably miffed because I addressed him as a dude, too. I wonder where Moses did get those stone tablets?

When I arrived home I entered through the garage. I went to my room, shut the door, and sprawled across my bed. I didn't feel much like talking to anybody, but then Jezi came out from under the bed, and we stared at each other nose to nose.

"Nobody understands, Jezi. I try to be helpful, and all I do is end up in trouble myself. I just feel like rolling over and playing dead.

Jezi cocked her head to one side, scratched her ear, and promptly rolled over on her back with her short little legs sticking straight up.

"Not you, silly dog! I appreciate your tricks, but I don't feel like laughing right now. I don't know why I feel so miserable. I didn't do a lick of work this afternoon."

Jezi scampered to me and licked me right in the face.

"You're not going to leave me alone, are you? Let's go fetch us some vittles, pooch."

Fetch to Jezi means to retrieve the spongy, chartreuse basketball I use to shoot through the tiny basket hanging from my closet door. Jezi scurried around looking for it, jumped on my bed, stuck her nose under my pillow, and came out with the ball clenched between her teeth. She looked up at me as if to say, "Excuse me, but are you looking for this?"

"You are certainly giving me the run-around, Jezi," I said, as we headed to the kitchen.

Sure enough, Jezi started running around in circles.

"Well, you have taken my mind off my problems and made me feel good again, Jezi. That has to be worth a treat."

Jezi sat up on her hind legs and barked — long and loud.

Filling her dish with food, I said, "You've earned this, my friend. I'm glad you don't know any more tricks. Why don't you perform like this when we have company?"

Patti came in when I was talking to Jezi and started razzing me. Luckily the phone rang, and she ran to answer it.

"Dad's going to be late," she said, and ran to tell Mom.

I made myself a peach milk shake knowing that dinner would be late again, and went back to my room to consume it. Seeing one of my puppets propped up in the chair by my computer, I remembered the speech meet was only a week away. I dug through the junk in my backpack to find my script. The puppet and I got comfortable on the bed and began rehearsing the lines. The script was a snap to learn. I basically had it all learned, but I needed to work on my movements with the puppet.

I fell asleep. A loud thunderclap awakened me. Rain was beating against the windowpanes and a strong wind was causing the branches of the trees near my room to brush against the house like a gigantic paint brush. I reached over to flick on the light beside my bed. Nothing happened. There was no power. Mom knocked on my door and entered before I answered. The beam of her flashlight caught me squarely in the eyes.

"Some storm, huh, PJ?" she asked. "Why are you sitting here in the dark, son?"

"I must've dozed off," I answered sleepily, covering my eyes against the glare of the flashlight.

"Well, come join the rest of the family and have a sandwich. The electricity will be off for quite awhile, so I just made tuna sandwiches," she said.

We dined by candlelight with Jezi getting more than her share of Patti's sandwich. Patti hates tuna. While we were eating, the conversation turned to Kent. I explained his latest episode — the fight in the classroom — and how he left school when someone told him the police were coming.

"So, what's happening to Kent now?" asked my dad.

"According to Gus, Kent is in juvenile hall right now. I don't know how long he will be there," I said.

Patti asked, "Does that mean he doesn't have to go to school?"

"No, honey, kids in juvenile hall go to school every day just like you do. They have very strict rules, do homework, and even have to make sure their rooms are clean. So, if you had some idea that juvenile hall is a vacation, forget it," said Dad.

Through the glass patio doors off our family room we watched streaks of lightning fill the sky.

"Dad, will we go on the field trip if it's raining tomorrow?" I asked.

"I'm sure we will," said Dad. "Some of the activities will be curtailed, like the tide pools and paddleboats, but the drivers can let you guys off right in front of the Aquarium so no one will get too wet if it is raining."

Thunder was so loud Patti covered her ears.

"Well, folks, there's at least one thing good about this situation," said Mom.

"What's that, Mom?" asked Dad.

"We don't have to do the dishes tonight!" she exclaimed.

I read my Bible by flashlight. Power was not restored and the rain continued to fall long after my head hit the pillow. I prayed for Kent, asking God to help him find himself and to be able to cope with all the problems in life.

Fortunately, power was restored during the night and it wasn't raining when Dad drove Patti and me to school.

The short ride to the Aquarium was uneventful. We met as a group outside the Aquarium where Mr. Bakker announced the teams that would be working together on a scavenger-hunt assignment and directed parent helpers to find a team and stay with them during the morning. Dad stayed with my team which included Gus, Hunt, Billy, Janelle, Lori, Theresa, and me.

"There's s-o-o-o much to find," said Lori, looking at the five-page assignment sheet.

"We'll never finish by lunch," said Gus.

Ever the optimist, I said, "Let's break this thing down and separate into small groups so we can cover the sections more quickly. Then we can meet back and compile all our answers."

"Good idea, PJ," said Janelle.

Gus and I headed for the third floor to find answers at the "Watching the Bay" section. Hunt and Billy went along with my dad to cover the second floor which included the Kelp exhibits and the Planet of the Jellies. The three girls stayed on the first floor. We had an inside tip that most of the information we needed was on the first floor, so the plan was for Gus and me to finish our area quickly and hustle back to help the girls.

"Why are we working so hard on this scavenger hunt?" I asked.

"Duh!" Where have you been? Don't you remember, PJ? Mr. Bakker promised a humongous pizza to the group that finds the most correct answers."

"I must've been in the office when that announcement was made. Seems like that's where I'm spending the better hours of my life lately. He probably won't pay up anyway. Come on, we've done all we can here," I remarked.

Two girls yelling at each other near the stairs attracted my attention. One of them threw a punch at the other one. In that split second I recognized Sybil and immediately ran to the rescue. I jumped right smack dab in the middle of that fight without even thinking about the consequences. My glasses went flying, but at least the girls stopped hitting each other.

Janie was crying. Sybil was fuming. That would have been a good time to make a wide sweep around them and just keep on trucking, but no, I always have to rush in where angels fear to tread.

"What's wrong with you guys?" I asked. "This is no way for two fine Christian ladies to behave."

"PJ, if I told you once, I've told you a zillion times . . . just mind your own business," Sybil shouted, trying to pull away from me. "Let go of my arm before I sock you."

"I just want to help. Promise me you'll stop hitting and I'll let go. Can't you guys solve your problem or at least leave it alone while we're on this field trip?" I asked. "What must people think when they see you fighting? It certainly isn't a very good testimony."

"Bug off, PJ!" Janie shouted.

"Yeah, who do you think you are, Mr. Holy Roller?" asked Sybil.

"Okay, I'll leave if you'll stop arguing and fighting," I promised.

"Well, fine!" huffed Sybil.

"Sure, sure!" agreed Janie, walking away.

"PJ, are you my friend?" asked Sybil.

"Sure, you know I am," I said.

"Okay, then now is your chance to prove it. What I want you to do is . . ."

CHAPTER FOURTEEN

SCAPEGOAT

For if you forgive men when they sin against you, your heavenly Father will also forgive you.

— Matthew 6:14

If you're really my friend, PJ, what I want you to do is tell everyone we're going together," said Sybil. She smiled and fluttered her eyelashes in a seductive way. Then she picked up my glasses, looked them over, and handed them back to me.

"Hah, hah, hah! That's the funniest thing I've heard all year," I said, doubling over and holding my side. Then I straightened up, put on my glasses, and adjusted them way down on my nose. I peered at her over the top of them like a nearsighted professor and said, "You're serious?"

"Of course, I'm very serious. You have to be serious, too. If you can't pull it off so everyone believes it, then just forget the whole thing," she said. "It's not like we have to make-out or anything. It would just be for show. You know, just for a few days."

"What do you hope to accomplish by telling people we're going together?" I asked.

"Well, what started this whole argument with Janie was that I told her some stuff about a guy I like, and she blabbed it all over. I can't believe she did that. I thought she was my friend. The thing is I really do like the guy, but I don't want him to think he owns me, and I really don't want my parents to find out about it. Know what I mean? So, if he finds out you and me are going together, he'll get jealous and . . . "

"Whoa, hold it right there! Sounds like you're setting me up to get pounded," I said.

"So, you got a problem with that?" Sybil laughed. "No, this guy isn't going to bother you, I promise."

"I'm not about to be a scapegoat, Sybil. Anyway, I don't see how all this is going to bring you and Janie back together," I said.

"Personally, I don't ever want to be her friend again. I can't trust her. If you promise to help me, I will at least leave her alone," said Sybil.

"Sounds too much like a soap opera to me. I'd like to help you, Sybil, but I really don't think your plan would work. How many girls do you know who have liked me as a boy friend?" I asked. "I'm like everyone's big brother."

"It will work, PJ. Don't you see, it's so unbelievable people will believe it," argued Sybil.

"Let it go, Sybil. I want to be your friend, but you're asking me to get involved in a shady deal that in all likelihood will backfire anyway," I said.

"So, you won't help me, is that it, PJ?" asked Sybil. "Fine friend you're turning out to be!"

"I won't help you in that way, but I'll help you and Janie get back together if you'll let me," I said.

"Yeah, right. Just forget it," she said, and stomped off.

I hurried downstairs to find Gus. The Aquarium was so crowded it was difficult to navigate around people. Gus and the others on our team weren't at the designated meeting place, so I went into the gift shop on the first floor. It seemed as if everyone from John Mark Christian School was packed into that gift shop. Billy was buying everything in sight, obviously without plan or purpose. Theresa was cuddling a two-foot stuffed black and white shark with its teeth bared. She would! Perfect match, I thought. Lori had purchased a small sea lion. It's funny how the things a person buys sort of match his/her personality. Then I spotted Gus who was just standing around with his hands in his pockets looking bored. Gus never had any money, but it didn't seem to bother him and he was a great moocher.

"Hey, where were you?" he asked. "We waited forever, and you never showed up."

"Sorry, dude. You should've stayed topside. You missed all the action between Janie and Sybil," I said. "Why'd you run off anyway?"

"Yeah, well, I didn't want to get involved. I don't need that kind of action, man. Those two are headed for big trouble if they don't get their act together. Why can't they just leave each other alone?" asked Gus. "You can be Batman to the rescue if you want, PJ, but leave me out of it."

"I wasn't too cool, I guess, but someone had to break up the fight. Did you guys find all the answers?" I asked, as we walked out of the gift shop.

"You gotta be kidding! We didn't even come close, but neither did any of the other groups. Everyone was copying from other groups and getting help from the volunteers at the information booths. It was funny. Mr. Bakker took up the sheets and gave us thirty minutes free time. Boy was he miffed. We're supposed to meet at the entrance and go have lunch," said Gus.

"Does that mean we didn't win the pizza?" I asked.

"Duh! Yeah, you might say that," said Gus, holding his chin reflectively.

The overcast sky gave every appearance of being ready to open up and rain all over us, so we quickly made our way to the nearest fast food establishment. The unannounced appearance of over forty junior-highers cheered up the manager but sent panic into the workers behind the counter. The parents and teachers congregated at one table to discuss our options for the remainder of the day. Gus and I sat in a booth close enough to hear what they were saying. "I'd say the paddleboats are out," said Mr. Cooper. "I doubt that the place is even open in this weather."

"Yeah, you're right," agreed Mr. Bakker. "But we could still go to the beach for awhile. It doesn't really matter if the sand is wet as long as it doesn't rain any more."

"Okay, let's finish eating and head 'em up and move 'em out," said Peggy's dad who looked every bit the part of a cowboy right out of a 1940's movie. He was wearing a ten-gallon hat and western boots with pointed toes. A toothpick hung loosely out the side of his mouth, and if I didn't know better, I would have sworn he was nursing a hunk of chewing tobacco.

We piled into the vehicles and headed for a stretch of beach at Lover's Point.

"Say, where is Mr. Cooper?" asked Dad, looking around. "Did he decide to ride to Lover's Point with someone else?"

"That's right, he was riding in front with you, Mr. Nichols. Maybe we left him behind," volunteered Gus.

"Well, we're almost at the beach. If he isn't there, I'll let you guys out and go back for him," announced my dad.

Evidently, several people had missed rides or purposely chosen to ride with someone else. Mr. Bakker had us stand still (no small miracle THAT) while he counted us. Mr. Cooper, Janie, Sybil, Lori, Maggie, Diana, Theresa, and her dad were unaccounted for. Mr. Bakker was losing it.

"Maybe I should call the police. Maybe something happened to them. Oh, my, what should I do?" he said, walking to and fro.

"Let's not panic yet, Mr. Bakker. Give them more time. I'll just bet they are all together and will be along before we know it," said my dad, doing his best to reassure Mr. Bakker.

The guys headed for the beach, but I remained behind with my dad to see if Mr. Cooper would show. I certainly hoped my dad was right, but I imagined all sorts of vile things happening to our lost group.

We waited for awhile and when the lost ones failed to show, we got into the van to double back to the Aquarium. As we were pulling out of our parking place, a van pulled up beside us. Mr. Cooper waved to us from the front seat. They parked and everyone on the missing list piled out and headed off as if nothing had happened.

I could tell that my dad was really relieved. Mr. Bakker came along and got right in Mr. Cooper's face, letting him know he was upset in no uncertain terms. Mr. Cooper was so cool.

"Sorry for the confusion. I was counseling with a couple of girls who were having some problems," stated Mr. Cooper matter-of-factly.

"I'm glad you guys showed up. PJ and I were going back to look for you," said my dad.

Mr. Bakker turned and walked away.

"Were Janie and Sybil the two girls?" I asked.

"PJ, that's really none of your business," said my dad.

"But I literally broke up a fight between them while we were in the Aquarium," I said.

My dad, Mr. Cooper, and I started walking toward the beach.

"That's okay, Mr. Nichols. Yes, PJ, Janie and Sybil were about to go at it again. They told me what you did. It all worked out, too. I sat down with the girls and asked them if they didn't want to talk to each other and work out the problem. At first they refused, but then I told them a story about my youngest son, the one who died recently, and a friend of his. These two grew up together and were the best of friends. Then in the first year of high school they had a serious disagreement about a beagle puppy Danny's friend Rich had given him. Danny wanted to give the puppy back because it kept chewing up everything, and Rich wouldn't take the puppy back. So Danny and I took the puppy to the animal shelter. Even before we left the shelter, a couple with a young child claimed the beagle. But Rich never forgave Danny for wanting to give the puppy back. They didn't speak to each other for well over a year, and the relationship never really healed after that. Both Danny and Rich graduated from high school. Rich went away to college and Danny joined the Army. I didn't see Rich again until my son's funeral. He came over to me with tears streaming down his cheeks and said, "I feel so badly because I never had a chance to tell Danny I was sorry for that argument we had over the dog. Now, I'll never get the chance."

Mr. Cooper hesitated, took out his handkerchief, and blew his nose. I could tell he was struggling.

"I told Janie and Sybil that story. They were both crying by the time I finished. Sybil walked over to Janie and knelt down by her. She told Janie she was sorry and asked for her forgiveness. God allowed me to witness a really special time in those girls' lives. I'll never forget it. They prayed, and they asked me to pray with them."

"Thank you for sharing that story, Mr. Cooper," my dad said.

"I'm sorry I caused everyone so much grief by being late and making the others late. Fortunately, Theresa's mom kept the other girls entertained while I talked to Janie and Sybil," said Mr. Cooper.

"Boy, I guess we take life for granted," said my dad. "You don't really know how precious life is and how quickly it can be snuffed out until you lose someone close to you. I'm so sorry about your son, Mr. Cooper. I firmly believe that the only one who can empathize with someone else is one who has experienced things like you have. God has really blessed these kids with a fine teacher. I'm convinced He sent you here to this place just to be an inspiration to them. I want to thank you right here in my son's presence for the positive influence you have had on him."

I just sort of drifted away from my dad and Mr. Cooper. They were still talking and evidently didn't notice when I left. I walked to the edge of the water and looked over toward the rocks where it seems most of our bunch had gathered. Most of the kids were climbing toward the highest point. As I walked over to begin my ascent to the top, I accidentally came upon Janie and Sybil sitting on a rock. They didn't see me, so for once I figured I would mind my own business and bypass them.

"Hey, PJ, come here!" shouted Sybil.

Uh-oh, now what, I thought. I hesitated for a brief moment and walked toward them, but I didn't say anything.

"Come sit down," said Sybil, patting the rock beside her.

"Yeah, we've got something to tell you," announced Janie.

"Do I want to hear it?" I asked, sitting beside Sybil in the spot she designated for me.

"PJ, aren't you curious as to why Janie and I are sitting here calmly without scratching each other's eyes out?" asked Sybil.

I shrugged my shoulders and played dumb.

"Well, you've told me to mind my own business so many times, I guess I've finally realized you mean it," I said.

"You're so sweet, PJ. Isn't he a peach, Janie? No, PJ, Janie and I are friends again. We made up. Isn't that just too cool?" asked Sybil.

I looked disbelievingly from one to the other, continuing my act.

"It's true, PJ," said Janie.

I had heard Mr. Cooper tell the whole story already, but I sat patiently as the girls related it to me again. They were both so emotional during the retelling that they began sobbing with me sitting right in the middle of it all. Frankly, I was having trouble with my own emotions. It was obvious to me that they had sincerely forgiven each other. For once I was part of something so wonderful I got a real warm feeling all over. My gushy feelings were shortlived, however, when I heard yelling and screaming coming from the rocky area.

"Someone better call 911!" shouted an oldtimer who had stopped on the beach near us to rest.

CHAPTER FIFTEEN

A CLASS ACT

A man's ways are directed by the Lord. How then can anyone understand his own way?

— Proverbs 20:24

The yelling emanated from the water's edge, not from the rocks as I had originally surmised. Janie, Sybil, and I took off running, but I soon outdistanced the girls. My first thought was that someone must've fallen or been pushed into the water and been caught in the undertow. I wondered if the oldtimer had really seen what happened, but I didn't stop to ask him. The rocky area was closer to help than where the girls and I were, so I didn't worry about calling 911 either. As it turned out, it would have been a false alarm anyway.

Over a dozen kids were clustered around something or somebody making it impossible to see what was happening. At this point, however, I could tell there was no emergency. Everyone was laughing and totally enthralled with whatever was going on at the center of the circle.

I inched my way forward, trying to get a clue as to why everyone was so excited. Never in my wildest dreams would I have believed what my eyes beheld.

"You better get me outta here, you hear! It's not funny any more," sputtered Gus, spitting out sand.

All I could see of Gus was his head. He was completely covered with sand from his neck down to his toes. Peggy, Diana, and Sandra were tickling Gus's nose while Dirk and Seth sat on him and tickled his feet.

I got down on my knees beside Gus and was about to ask him a few questions about the situation when Mr. Bakker came along.

"What's going on here? You guys break it up!" he bellowed, coming into the center of the circle.

"Oh my goodness!" he exclaimed when he saw Gus buried in the sand. "Get off of him and get him out of there immediately. You guys are really, really in trouble now. I might've known you would be right in the middle of this, PJ," he said, looking straight at me.

Before I could say a word, Diana said, "Don't jump to conclusions, Mr. Bakker. PJ wasn't involved in any way. He just got here."

Mr. Bakker's face was as red as a beet, and it wasn't from being sunburned either. "We'll just see about that. I want the names of everyone who was even standing here," he demanded.

Of course, most everyone had scattered to the four winds, and the memories of those few still standing there suddenly became very fuzzy. Gus was out of the sand and trying desperately to wipe all the sand off.

"Come on, Gus, let's go get you cleaned up in the restroom," I said, grabbing his shoes and pulling him by the arm.

"You haven't heard the last of this, PJ," said Mr. Bakker.

That wasn't the end of our troubles for the day either. We were supposed to return to school by around 3:00 p.m. so that kids whose parents picked them up wouldn't have to wait. As we were driving back to school, the van suddenly lurched to the right. My dad gripped the wheel tighter, pulled over on the shoulder, and rolled to a jerky stop.

"Well, guys, looks like we have a flat," said my dad, matter-of-factly.

I looked out through the rain-covered window and thought of the verse in the Bible where it says that God allows the rain to fall on the just and the unjust. My dad was so cool. He didn't fly off into a rage. He didn't curse or blame God. I silently prayed and asked God to help my dad and to let the rain stop.

"I'll have to ask you guys to share the rain with me. I can't jack the van up with all of your excess weight," he said laughing. "PJ, see if you can find a large rock to put behind the rear wheels. Maybe Mr. Cooper can help you. I'll have this thing repaired in a jiffy. You other guys go stand over there under that tree and try to keep dry."

After Mr. Cooper and I had scotched the wheels as my dad directed, I remained close beside him in case he needed me. Mr. Cooper went over to keep an eye on the gang.

As Dad labored to loosen the lug nuts, he said, "I don't know what happened. These tires are like new. We must've run over a nail or something. The tire went flat so quickly, it was almost like having a blowout."

When he took the tire off the rim, I rolled it around slowly and found that not one but several silver-colored nailheads had pierced the tire. I pointed them out to my dad.

"Do you think someone purposely threw a lot of nails on the road?" I asked.

"It's possible. Guess we'll never know, son. Thanks for your help. Go round up the guys and let's get going," he said.

The rain had slowed down to a trickle by the time the van was up on the jack. It took my dad less than ten minutes to change the tire. Then we loaded up and were on our way again.

By visiting the Aquarium in the middle of the week, we had avoided the heavy rush of tourists that invade the place on weekends. I thought about the things that happened on the field trip as we drove back to school. Sybil and Janie had settled their differences. Mr. Bakker would probably make my life miserable in the days to come because he thought I buried Gus in the sand. With a multitude of kids around Gus, I was the only one he seemed to blame. Billy and everyone else spent all their money on meaningless things. But the best part of the trip was spending time with my dad. I really admire him and hope that I can be exactly like him someday. Easter recess was two days away, and Friday was designated as a minimum day, so I figured any idiot could make it without getting into too much trouble.

At the awards assembly on Thursday morning, Mr. Cramer presented certificates to the students who made the Honor Roll and Principal's List for top grades. I think the entire junior high went into shock when he called my name.

"All right, PJ!" exclaimed Gus, who was sitting beside me. Gus stood up and we slapped hands like the pro's do as I exited the pews and headed for the stage.

I took my time going forward, strutting and greeting my fans on both sides of the aisle along the way. After all, it was expected of me. Having attended John Mark Christian School since preschool, I had a reputation to uphold. Mr. Cramer was waiting for me with his arms folded.

"Glad you could make it, PJ," he said.

"No problem, Sir."

Mr. Cramer doesn't normally stop to chat with everyone who gets an award. I figured he was up to something. I stood directly beside him while still facing the baptistery and did a perfect military about face.

"At ease, compadre," Mr. Cramer commanded.

I gave him my hung-dog look and slouched low with my arms hanging limp.

"I said 'at ease', not hang loose," he laughed.

The audience was cracking up.

I stood stone-faced, staring at Mr. Cramer, waiting for him to say something. Mr. Cramer held the microphone up to say something but started laughing every time he tried to speak. Then he held it in front of me for me to say something, and I just stood there silently, planted like a tree.

Finally, he said, "So, you are an honor student this quarter. How many times during your academic career has this honor been bestowed upon you?"

I held my right hand up in front of me with my fingers spread as widely apart as I could and began counting each finger. I had folded four fingers down when Mr. Cramer interrupted me.

"Are you going to need to take your shoes and socks off?" he asked.

I ignored him and finished my counting. Turning to face him, I said, "None, Sir, but I had perfect attendance in kindergarten."

"Well, I'd like to continue this interview, but others are waiting. Nice work, PJ, and keep it up until the end of the year. The secretary tells me you are the first junior high boy to make the Honor Roll in two years."

Spontaneously, I reached over and threw my arms around Mr. Cramer, giving him a big hug. Then I began skipping down the aisle back to the junior high section with my award certificate held high above my head.

When we returned to our room after the assembly, Mr. Cooper gave us the remainder of our English class time to practice for the speech meet. Janie, Janelle, Jon, and I had written an original puppet script and had practiced it over and over. Our puppet show, written mostly by Janelle, is about two junior high guys who think a Christian is someone who goes to church every Sunday, attends youth group, and doesn't beat up on people. The two girls in the play are able to convince the boys that a Christian is someone whom God has changed from the inside. After several funny scenes, the girls encounter each boy separately and lead them to the Lord. Mr. Cooper let us perform our puppet show to the kids in kindergarten and first grade. It was a big hit, but we have performed so often we were getting sick of it.

"Mr. Cooper, since we know our skit so well, may we study for our math test?" asked Janelle.

"I want everyone to go through their speech once. Your group can go first and then you can have free time," said Mr. Cooper. "The speech meet is on Friday after Easter recess. Everyone needs to polish his act so that it's perfect. This year all of you are going to win. I feel it in my bones."

"Sure, right, Mr. Cooper. You said that last year, too!" exclaimed Amy, who was about as perfect as anyone could be when reciting a poem called "The Highwayman."

After we performed for the class, I packed the four puppets

into the suitcase and parked it in the storage closet. My dad had allowed me to use these four puppets because he and I were not using them for any of the shows we were rehearsing for Sunday school. I had to do some fast talking to get them, and my dad let me know in no uncertain terms that the puppets' safekeeping was in my hands. The closet in Mr. Cooper's room remains locked, so I felt fairly safe leaving them at school.

When Theresa finished saying her speech, "The First Day of School," I quickly approached Mr. Cooper and asked to be excused. As I was walking slowly toward the restroom the thought entered my mind that I might get lucky. Maybe this would be the day I would catch the person who had been writing on the wall in the restroom. It was as if catching that guy was my mission in life. The whole thing had almost become an obsession with me, and there wasn't even a reward. Boy, am I some sort of nut, or what, I thought.

As I walked toward the restroom, Rachel, a fifth grader who was known around school for her scatterbrained antics, darted around the corner of the building and was about to enter the boys restroom when she saw me. I mean, she had the door open and was halfway inside!

Seeing me, Rachel said, "Oops, silly me! Now, how did I do that? I almost went into the boys restroom." She was still laughing when she walked into the female counterpart.

The first thing I did was check to see if there was any new writing on the wall. I was disappointed at not finding any. In fact, the custodian, Mr. Arnold, had repainted the entire wall which had been so badly defaced. I had a funny feeling in the pit of my stomach. Could it be that Rachel was the one who had been writing and drawing on the walls all this time? That's crazy, I thought. Boys are always coming and going. It would take a pretty gutsy girl to attempt something like that. The chances of a girl being caught inside, especially with the high alert Mr. Cramer had on catching the person, were pretty great indeed. As I thought further about it though, Rachel might just have enough guts to do something stupid like that. A girl! It was almost beyond comprehension. I walked out of the restroom and jogged over to hide behind the dumpster nearby. From that vantage point I hoped to entrap Rachel, so convinced was I that she was the guilty party. I figured she would come out of the girls restroom and proceed immediately to the boys restroom to do her dirty work. I had interrupted her, and if my hunch was correct, wild horses couldn't keep her from her mission.

Mr. Arnold came out of the kitchen which is located in the sanctuary building carrying two large black bags, one over each shoulder. Setting the bags down, he lifted the heavy dumpster lid, letting it fall backwards toward the chain-link fence. I was at the opposite end of the dumpster out of his view. When that lid came crashing down above my head, I thought the rapture had come.

"Whoa!" I yelled. "You almost got me, Mr. Arnold."

"PJ, what in the world are you doing behind the dumpster?" he asked. Don't tell me you're doing some kind of science project for Mr. Bakker. You gotta have a better excuse than that for me not to take you to the principal.'

"It's a long story, Mr. Arnold. I was trying to catch the person who has been writing on the wall in the restroom, so I hid behind the dumpster," I said.

Mr. Arnold scratched his head. He didn't look too convinced.

"No, really. I think I know who's been doing the damage in there, and I almost caught her in the act a few minutes ago," I stated.

"Her? You think a girl has been doing it?" asked Mr. Arnold. "That's crazy. A girl would have to be pretty brazen to even try something that far out. Just out of curiosity, let's you and me make a visit to the restroom to see if our resident artist has been at work again."

My knees grew weak as we walked the short distance to the restroom. What if my hunch was right and Rachel had sneaked into the restroom while Mr. Arnold and I were chatting by the dumpster? She could've etched out a few sketches and left unnoticed. Mr. Arnold would think I had done it.

"Well, let's see what we have here," said Mr. Arnold, as he pushed open the door allowing me to walk in ahead of him.

CHAPTER 16

THERESA UPSTAGED

Be careful not to do your acts of righteousness before men, to be seen by them. If you do, you will have no reward from your Father in heaven.

— Matthew 6:1

The wall was clean. "Now isn't that the neatest paint job you've ever seen?" asked Mr. Arnold. "but then it should be. Lord knows I've had enough practice painting it. I was wrong, PJ. I gotta admit, I thought I had caught the culprit. I thought you messed up my freshly-painted wall and was hiding behind the dumpster 'cause you saw me coming. Sorry, PJ. I was about to falsely accuse you."

"Yeah, I guess everyone thinks I'm guilty. I always seem to be in the wrong place at the wrong time," I said. "I better get back to class, Mr. Arnold. See ya later."

"Stay outta trouble, young man," he called after me.

I had been wrong about Rachel, or else she was clever enough to know how close she had come to being caught. She was one I would definitely add to my growing list of suspects.

My time in math class was cut short because Gus and I had signed up to work the bake sale. Every Friday for the entire school year the seventh and eighth graders bring goodies to sell to the students as they leave the lunch room. The first shift, which Gus and I were working, has the most action. All of the fifth and sixth graders invade like a horde of locusts. They buy and consume everything in sight. Mr. Cooper finally agreed to let us hold some of the good stuff back for our group; otherwise, it would be all gone by our lunch time. Monies earned from the bake sale go into a fund for the junior high Washington D.C. trip. Each one of us has a separate account, so when we work on any project like washing cars, candy sales, gift wrapping sales, or bake sales the money is divided equally and credited to our accounts. With the "granny" letters I mailed out hitting up all my relatives for donations, I have practically paid for my entire trip.

"Find anything interesting written on the wall in the restroom, PJ?" asked Rachel, who stood before me to buy something.

"Funny you should ask," I said. "Were you going to work on your mural some more when I came along and interrupted you?"

"NO way!" she exclaimed. "I just made an honest mistake. I was concentrating so hard, I wasn't looking where I was going."

"Sure, sure, and my friend Gus here plays with a rubber ducky in the bathtub. Say, if you would like a guided tour of the boys restroom, Rachel, I'll talk to Mr. Cramer about arranging one," I teased.

"Nah, if you've seen one, you've seen 'em all," she said.

"Trust me on this, little girl. If you are the one who is messing up the wall, your days are numbered. I'm going to catch you, just wait and see," I threatened.

Rachel smirked and walked away eating a chocolate cupcake.

Theresa and Tanya relieved Gus and me so we could eat our lunch. All of our classes were shortened since it was the last day before our Easter break. Gus and I gobbled down our food as fast as possible in order to give us more time to shoot hoops. Finding all the courts taken, Gus and I convinced Dirk and Jose to let us play with them. Before long, we succeeded in making them mad enough to leave. According to plan, of course. Then Gus and I got down to some serious shooting.

"So, what are you doing during vacation?" asked Gus.

"I got a couple of major things going on," I responded. "First, I'm running a 5K race tomorrow. Then on Monday, my sister and I are flying to Colorado to visit my grandparents on their ranch. We'll be spending the entire week there. It's going to be a blast even if I do have to put up with my little sister for a few days."

"Wow, boy are you lucky! I have to get up early every day and deliver my stupid newspapers. Sometimes I really hate that job," lamented Gus.

Gus made a hook shot from outside the key near the free-throw line. I retrieved the ball and attempted the same shot.

After missing the shot, I said, "No rest for the wicked. What can I say? Just think of all the money you make. It must be nice."

"Aw, I don't make that much, and then I go blow it on stupid arcade games and junk. Like today after school, you know. I'm supposed to meet Kent at the arcade. I'll probably blow $20.00 and have nothing to show for it," said Gus.

Gus dribbled under the basket and made an over-the-head shot without even looking.

"Sounds like fun, man," I said.

I missed the shot. The first one to spell HORSE would be out.

"You have an 'R' now," Gus reminded me. "Why don't you come along?"

"I don't know. I probably shouldn't. Kent hasn't called me, and I haven't been around him in quite awhile," I said. "In fact, the last time I saw Kent, his brother had just beat him up. Kent was really a mess. My mom called Pastor Bob and asked if the incident should be reported to the Child Abuse Agency or something. If Kent found out my mom did that, it's no wonder he hasn't called me."

"Well, I've seen Kent a couple of times since he got out of juvenile hall, and he didn't say anything about his brother, your mom, or you," said Gus. "He did mention that he was meeting with Pastor Bob, but I thought that was just because they are friends."

Gus missed a long shot from behind the key giving me the opportunity to go on the offensive. I dribbled to the side of the court, turned, and shot. The ball swished through the hoop without touching the rim.

"Good one!" acknowledged Gus.

He missed the shot by a mile, and before I could get another one off, the bell rang.

"So, we're tied with an "R" apiece. We'll have to finish the game later. I haven't got anything else to do this afternoon. Maybe I will meet you at the arcade," I said, as we walked back to class.

During creative writing Mr. Cooper gave those who wanted an opportunity to rehearse their speeches again. Amy's hand was up first, and she's already the best hope we have for winning a trophy this year. I've heard her give "The Highwayman" so many times, I almost have it memorized myself. Maggie went through her speech named "Baseball" without missing a word. Mr. Cooper was fairly beaming by the time Theresa's turn came. Theresa had one of the longest and most difficult speeches to learn. I don't think she has ever said the whole thing without messing up.

"Good job, Theresa," said Mr. Cooper. "You almost have it."

"Yeah, sure! Give me a millennium and I'll win for sure," Theresa said, evidently very upset with herself.

"Don't give up, Theresa. You have one of the funniest speeches. After Easter break I'll let you work in the library with someone every day until you get it. It's going to be great. Go through it once more. We have time," said Mr. Cooper.

When Theresa started through her lines again, I began playing around with my puppet. This puppet, named Wilfred, is as ugly as sin, which is one reason why I suppose my dad let me bring it to school. I had Wilfred perched on my hand, and whenever Theresa messed up or said a funny line (which was quite often in her speech), I gave Wilfred free rein. Wilfred really put on a show, upstaging Theresa at every turn.

Theresa stopped in mid-sentence, planted one foot firmly in front of the other, placed her hands on her hips, and truly portrayed the role of the schoolmarm in her speech.

"PJ, if you don't stop that this instance, I'm going to come over there and snatch that puppet right out of your hands," she thundered through clinched teeth.

Wilfred was resting placidly on the desk.

I gave Theresa my you-mean-sweet-little-old-me look and hunched my shoulders as if to say, "But I'm innocent, dear. I don't have the foggiest idea what you are talking about."

"PJ, try to hold it together. This is serious, and Theresa really needs the practice," said Mr. Cooper.

Then Theresa glared at Mr. Cooper for seeming to imply that she was so awful.

Mr. Cooper picked up on her look and said, "I didn't mean it that way, Theresa. Go ahead, you're doing great."

Everyone was watching me to see what I would do. Mr. Cooper glanced in my direction but saw Wilfred lying peacefully on the desk and quickly focused his attention back on Theresa. Wilfred inched himself up ever so slowly. He pretended to take something out of Cheryl's hair, looked at it, shook his head, and threw the pretend-thing away. Then he repeated the same thing, but this time he placed the pretend-morsel in his mouth and began chewing vigorously. Cheryl, sitting in front of me, had no idea what was happening behind her back. A few guys sitting close enough to see what I had done cracked up.

Theresa froze. Her body became rigid with her arms hanging straight down and her fists clinched. She didn't say a word. She didn't need to; the look on her face said it all. I had gone too far. Fortunately the bell rang, so I hastily stuffed Wilfred into my desk, grabbed my backpack off the floor, and bolted for the door.

"Not so fast, PJ. Go back to your seat," commanded Mr. Cooper.

I figured I would get the big lecture in front of the whole class for my shenanigans.

"Let's bow our heads and pray that God will give us a safe vacation and that we will spend time worshipping Him and remembering Christ's death, burial, and resurrection during this Easter time. Bow your heads, close your eyes, and pray with me," directed Mr. Cooper.

Following the prayer, I got out of there as fast as I could, but it wasn't fast enough. Theresa was right behind me. She grabbed me by the arm, swung me around, and got right in my face. Boy, is she strong!

"What's the big idea, PJ?" she bellowed.

She was acting all tough, but I could see tiny tears in the corner of her eyes. I realized that I had really hurt her feelings. It was time to be cool. I have witnessed several arguments between my mom and dad, so I am somewhat knowledgeable about how to play the game.

"I'm sorry, Theresa. I just got carried away. I know what I did was wrong, and I certainly didn't mean to hurt you. I just enjoy entertaining people, I was bored, and you . . . "

Theresa interrupted me, saying, "Yeah, me. You used me as your bait. Well, I don't appreciate being made fun of so you can entertain people. What you did was downright rude."

"I'm really sorry, Theresa. If you want, I'll apologize in front of the whole class."

I wanted to end the conversation and be on my way to meet Gus and Kent at the mall.

"Just forget it, okay? I know the class wasn't laughing at me. They were watching you and that silly puppet. I guess I'm just jealous because you had the class so totally absorbed in your little act. What I wouldn't give to have a little of your talent," she said. She wiped at her eyes and smiled.

Sensing that we had turned a corner, I said, "Shucks, ma'am, it ain't nuthin'. Theresa, I'll help you with your speech after vacation if you want. It's the least I can do."

"I'm that bad, huh?" she said, laughing. "Thanks, PJ. I'll take you up on that."

She leaned over and hugged me, totally catching me off guard. She had to lean over because she is so tall, and I'm almost two feet shorter than she is.

I could feel my face turning red, but I quickly turned away and made tracks to the bike rack.

I went by the house to drop my books off and tell my mom

where I was going. Shedding my school uniform like a snake sheds its skin, I changed into jeans and a T-shirt. No more uniform for almost two weeks, I thought.

At the mall, I found Gus standing at his favorite video game. I looked around for Kent, but didn't see him. Gus was so involved in the game, he didn't even acknowledge my presence. I stood beside him watching silently until he messed up.

"Where's Kent?" I asked.

"Don't know. He was supposed to meet me here almost an hour ago," Gus said. He inserted another token into the slot and started a new game.

"I'm going to play the Intrudor over there," I said. "Come get me when you're ready to go."

"Okay, dude. If Kent doesn't show up soon, I'm not going to stay around here very long," said Gus.

I was still on my first game when Gus came over.

"Want to get a coke after you finish this game, PJ," he asked.

"Sure, that's cool," I responded.

I already had top score of the day, so I purposely messed up to end the game.

As we walked past the pay telephone booths, Gus said, "I think I'll give Kent a call. I have a feeling something has happened, or he would've been here."

CHAPTER SEVENTEEN

ON VACATION

My times are in your hands.

— Psalm 31:15

As I pedaled home I thought about Kent and made up my mind that I would call him when I returned from Colorado. I realized I hadn't been a very good friend to Kent, and I silently asked God to forgive me and help me make it right. As I reflected about the past few weeks, I came to the realization that I was reverting to the old PJ, the one who enjoyed being a clown no matter what and no matter whom I hurt. Theresa was a prime example. Maybe during vacation I can get my act together, I thought. I certainly didn't want to resume my old role as class clown.

Saturday morning I woke up at 7:15 a m (with a little help from my mom). I dressed in my running shorts, a T-shirt from the last race I had run, my Nike Air shoes, and headed for the kitchen.

Patti was already dressed and sat at the table feeding her face. With a mouthful of crackling, nutless fruity-o's, she mumbled, "You're gonna be late."

"What time does the race begin?" asked my mom.

"Eight o'clock. I need to hurry. At least I'm pre-registered, so all I have to do is pick up my race packet. Can we leave now?" I asked.

"Just as soon as you eat your breakfast, young man."

"Aw, Mom, you know I don't eat before a race. I'll eat after, I promise," I said.

Jezi who always seems to know when we're getting ready to go somewhere, was sitting by the door waiting patiently.

"Okay, Jezi You can go, too, but you'll have to stay on your leash," announced my mom. "Patti, please pick up Jezi and bring her along."

Most of the runners were at the starting area by the time I picked up my race packet. I managed to get in a few stretching exercises just before the announcer called all the runners to the starting line. I looked around but failed to see anyone I knew. I noticed that there were very few kids running the 5K. Both 5K and 10K runners started at the same time. The field of runners was small. Even though I had planned to take it fairly easy and use this race as a practice for the Big Sur 5K which was coming up in a few weeks, I really wanted to win. As I surveyed the field trying to calculate my chances of winning, I saw Miss Puffer, the sixth grade teacher at John Mark Christian School. She was lined up at the back of the pack of runners.

"Oh, you-who PJ," she called.

I made my way back to where she was standing. "Hello, Miss Puffer. Why are you standing back here? You should be up front with all the other fast runners."

Several people around us laughed. There I go again, I thought. Even without trying I make people laugh.

"Oh, you silly boy. At my age I get my inspiration by running at the back of the pack. That way I can keep an eye on the good-looking fellas," she laughed.

Some guys standing near us took a good look at Miss Puffer and laughed, not at her but with her. She winked and smiled coyly.

"Good luck, Miss Puffer," I said, as I began snaking my way through the slower runners.

Mrs. Puffer was running right beside me.

"You're setting a mighty stiff pace for an older lady, PJ," she said, but it was evident that she wasn't laboring to keep up with me.

I figured I would out-distance her soon, or that she would become too tired and drop back. Wrong! Miss Puffer stayed right with me for the entire three and two-tenths miles. I didn't know whether to be upset or happy. Here I was fifty or a hundred years younger than she and she was beating the pants off me.

We were running slightly downhill as we rounded the final turn and headed for the finish line. Miss Puffer matched my pace stride for stride. With two blocks to go, Miss Puffer started pulling away from me.

"See you at the finish, PJ," she called.

I'm not going to let a little old lady beat me. Not on your life! I lengthened my stride, took deeper breaths and caught up with Miss Puffer. One block to go. I could read the numerals on the digital clock as we approached the finish line. The crowd, small as it was, saw a dramatic finish developing between Miss Puffer and me and began yelling excitedly.

"Come on, PJ, you can do it." It was my mom, I could tell that voice anywhere.

"Go, PJ, go. Don't let her catch you!" yelled Patti.

I even heard Jezi barking.

I was ever so slightly ahead of Miss Puffer and kicking for the finish line with every ounce of strength I could muster.

24:03 flashed on the clock.

I did it! I beat Miss Puffer, and I was as proud of that as if I had just won a major race in the Olympics.

"Nice job, PJ. I'll get you next time," said Miss Puffer. She wasn't breathing as hard as I was, and for a moment I wondered, "Had she let me beat her on purpose?"

At the awards ceremony, both Miss Puffer and I won first place medals in our respective divisions. I was really surprised when a photographer for the local newspaper asked us to pose for a picture together. He recorded our names, we answered his questions, and he told us the story would appear in Sunday's paper.

Fortunately neither Patti nor my mom mentioned the fact that an old lady just about beat me in the race. I was proud of my medal but didn't say a word about it under the circumstances.

Miss Puffer had really done me a favor. I had to exert myself more to stay up with her and as a result established a new PR (personal best).

Jezi got under my feet, as I moved about the room packing my suitcase with all the paraphernalia I couldn't do without in Colorado. I took all the usual stuff like underwear, socks, shirts, and pants, but I also packed my Walkman TV, comic books, headphones, tons of candy, gum, playing cards, and my Bible.

As I was zipping up my bag my mom came in and asked "Did you pack your toothbrush and deodorant?"

Without saying a word I marched into the bathroom to retrieve the items I had forgotten.

"How about your swim suit? Did you remember that?" she asked.

I rummaged through my drawers until I found a faded blue suit which I added to my bag and again started to zip it up.

"Did you remember to pack a jacket, PJ? It can get pretty cold in Aurora this time of year."

"I'll bet you didn't pack your shaving stuff, big brother," said Patti.

I had to admit Patti had done pretty well up until that outburst. She had been standing quietly beside Mom waiting for me to finish so we could leave for the airport.

"Give it a rest Patti! I'm doing the best I can." I said.

I unzipped my bag for the umpteenth time and walked to my closet to get a jacket. Jezi jumped up on my bed, hopped right into my bag on top of all my things, and laid down with her head between her front paws. Leave it to Jezi to punctuate a tense moment with her own brand of humor.

"No, Jezi. I'm not taking you with me. You need to stay home and guard the fort," I said, putting her back on the carpet.

"Can we go now?" asked Patti.

"But of course, my dear," I said, brushing my hair back with the palm of my hand and swaggering toward Patti with my suitcase in the other hand.

When we boarded the plane, Patti had to have the window seat, and rather than create a scene, I reluctantly consented to the arrangement. My unselfish gesture evoked audible words or praise and adulation from a couple sitting beside us just across the aisle.

"What a nice young man. You are indeed fortunate to have such a wonderfully kind brother, little one," she said to Patti.

I flashed all my teeth, braces and all.

Patti politely said, "Thank you, ma'am," but then she faced the window and stuck out her tongue.

Since I was seated next to the lady with only a tiny aisle separating us, it was my lot to listen to her endless babble, Her husband had no doubt learned that napping was the best way to avoid his wife's chatter. His act, if it was an act, was so real that it was punctuated by snoring for which the little lady apologized countless times. During the course of our flight, I learned more than I ever wanted to know about the couple's travels to Russia, China, Australia, Africa Mexico, Europe and Texas. I had only myself to blame since I smiled and was so friendly.

The lady finally took a break, excused herself, and waddled down the aisle toward the toilet facilities.

"Patti, Patti, you gotta change seats with me!" I begged.

Patti was leaning back on a small, white pillow about the size of a Texas handkerchief. "Why, PJ?" she asked. "I like it here better."

I glanced furtively down the aisle and back to the lady's empty seat. Her husband had his eyes closed, but I could've sworn he smiled.

"I'll do anything. Just name it," I offered in desperation.

Patti perked up. "Will you take me with you wherever you go while we're on vacation?" she asked.

The thought totally sickened me. but since we were going to a foreign land where no one knew me, I figured it would be okay, and besides, she would soon tire of tagging along with me. I had ways of making sure of that.

"Deal," I said. scooting in her direction before she changed her mind.

I should've calculated the flight time more accurately. By the time the lady was back in her seat the captain announced that we were cleared to land at the Denver airport. I wondered if Patti realized the flight was almost over when she evoked that promise from me. Now for the next five days I was indentured to a pint-sized squirt. Maybe she would forget, I thought. I looked in her direction. She was smiling. What a brat! No way was she going to forget. She knew exactly what she had done.

After the ordeal on the plane, I was ready for a hot shower and a soft bed. Luckily our grandparents were waiting for Patti and me when we deplaned. After hugs and greetings all around we drove from the airport to my grandparent's ranch on the outskirts of Aurora.

"You gonna get up at the crack of dawn and help me milk the cows and do the chores PJ?" asked Granddad, as he pulled our suitcases out of the trunk of the car when we leached our destination.

"Say what?" I asked. "I'm on vacation. I plan to sleep late, go swimming in the lake, ride Whinny . . . you still have Whinny, don't you?"

"Yeah, ol' Whinny and several more quarter horses," said Granddad.

"Remember I get to go with you wherever you go," said Patti, as she turned and headed into her room at the top of the stairs.

"Okay, Granddad, Patti and I will be glad to milk the cows at 5:30 a.m.," I said loudly enough for Patti to hear me.

"Oh no, I'm not getting up in the middle of the night to milk cows. I don't even like milk. I'll let you off this time, PJ," said Patti.

"No way, Patti, we agreed that you would go everywhere I went while we're here. We have a deal for the whole trip or no deal at all," I said.

"Oh, all right. You think you're so smart! I don't want to go everywhere with you anyway," said Patti.

"Yes! Thank you, Lord," I exclaimed.

Granddad who had been listening to our little conversation, said, "Well, it's settled then. I'll see you at 5:00 a.m. sharp, PJ."

I detected the hint of a smile.

CHAPTER EIGHTEEN

THERESA GETS IT TOGETHER

All a man's ways seem right to him, but the Lord weighs the heart.

— Proverbs 21 2

Sunlight streaming through the window beside my bed struck me on the face startling me from a deep sleep. I sat straight up. rubbing my eyes. and wondering why the lady on the plane was shining a flashlight in my face. To my surprise, there was no lady. The digital clock on the bedside table read 9:38. I had slept half the morning, something I rarely did. I was dreaming about my ordeal with the lady on the plane and remembered all too well the scene just before I woke up. The lady was dressed in a fur coat, but beneath it she was wearing a blue and white striped bikini. She kept arguing with her husband about being hot and telling him she was going to take of her coat and could care less what he said. When the bright sunlight awakened me, I thought the man said in a squeaky voice, "You do that and we're through!" Trying to analyze my own dream I realized my image of the flashlight, the lady's fur coat, and the heat she was experiencing all came from the sun shining through the window on me. What the man said could've been one of my granddad's roosters. It was a weird dream. I just hope I never see a grandmotherly-type lady on the beach wearing a blue and white bikini.

I must've been a sight to Grandma when I sauntered into the kitchen wearing my navy blue sweatsuit pants, a white T-shirt, no shoes, and with my uncombed hair going every which way.

"Well, PJ did you finally decide to join the land of the living?" asked Grandma. "What would you like for breakfast?"

Yawning I said, "I think I'll skip breakfast. I can't believe I slept so long. Why didn't Grandpa wake me?"

"You're probably experiencing jet lag, honey. I have some homemade biscuits in the oven, and I'll bet you can't eat just one. Granddad tried to wake you up; maybe not too much of a try, but I know he called you same as he did Patti." said Grandma. "Patti got right up and went out to do the chores with your granddad."

Grandma sat two steaming hot biscuits in front of me. Butter and blackberry jam were already on the table. How could I resist?

"Patti got up at 5:30 a.m.? I can't believe it," I said.

✥

"Oh my lands, no! It wasn't 5:30. It was more like 7:30. Your granddad was snoring up a storm at 5:30 a.m.," said Grandma. Granddad was only kidding you when he asked you to get up at 5:30 to help milk the cows. Why, we have milking machines to do that and the chores are mostly done by our hired help. Patti and your granddad are out having a gay old time right now, so quit your worrying about not getting up sooner."

I consumed the two biscuits Grandma had given me and two more besides.

What a life! I didn't see Patti until late in the day. After making a pig of myself at breakfast I dressed more appropriately and went out to explore. Granddad's barn is like a museum. The huge steel structure actually doesn't resemble a barn at all. It's more like a humongous warehouse with half of it filled with all sorts of antiques. The other half, partitioned off with a five-foot high wall, was like a real barn with stalls for horses, cows, and assorted types of other animals. I always head for the barn first when we visit because of the antiques. Over the years different things in the barn have attracted my attention. Granddad's old Lionel train collection held my interest when I was younger. My focus last summer was the jukebox loaded with songs from the 1950's and an old pinball machine with buttons on each side which are used to move the levers that propel the steel balls along their way. Collecting things (junk my grandma calls it) is an obsession with my granddad. I could always count on finding something new to occupy my time.

In the corner, covered with a heavy green tarpaulin, was a 1929 Ford coupe. I carefully pulled the tarp up enough to view the front of the classic. The Ford was completely restored with a glossy black finish and chrome that sparkled. As I reached down to pull the tarp farther back so I could see the interior of the car, I was bowled over by something or someone behind me.

"Whoa!" I yelled, getting to my feet and staring at the blackest billygoat I had ever seen. "Where did you come from, bud?"

"Baa, baaa," came the reply.

"There you are, Cornelius. I've been looking all over for you," said Patti. She ran up to the black goat and threw her arms around it.

"Friend of yours?" I asked, brushing off my pants. Fortunately, Patti had not witnessed Cornelius's sneak attack.

Patti noticed that the tarp on the old Ford was pulled back and said, "Aw, umm, PJ, I'm going to tell Granddad you've been messing with his baby."

"What d'ya mean? Looking doesn't do any harm. Besides, I'll bet Grandpa will even let me drive it next year when I turn fourteen."

"Fat chance, buster. Grandpa told me this very morning that he doesn't even drive this car. He just hauls it on a trailer to the car shows," said Patti. "It's worth a lot of money." It wasn't worth arguing about, not with my little sister. I carefully replaced the tarp and headed for the door. Patti and the goat were right behind me.

It's been such a neat day, Lord, please don't mess it up now. I prayed.

Patti and Cornelius peeled off and went towards the pasture. I spend the rest of the afternoon lying in a hammock strung between two shade trees in back of the house. I had uncovered a collection of old comic books up in the loft in the barn. Taking a stack from the box, I grabbed myself a snack from the fridge and settled down to read. I thought I had died and gone to heaven with all those Batman, Superman, and Captain Marvel comics. I handled them very gingerly because I knew they were expensive.

Grandma came out and started rocking the hammock back and forth. She said. "We're going out to a nice restaurant and then to a concert this evening, PJ. Won't that be fun?"

It's funny how you remember all the pleasant happy times you have experienced but tend to block out memories of those things you found unpleasant. When I was in third grade I visited my grandparents and was formally introduced to a symphony orchestra. I made such a pest of myself that time, I figured my point was made and no one would ever take me to another such performance. It was indeed a terrible scene. An usher came to the section where we were seated and told my granddad that I was making faces at the members of the orchestra and if my antics continued we would be asked to leave. That's the only time in my life I have ever seen Granddad show any anger. He was furious but he made his point without resorting to any form of physical abuse. I don't remember what he said when he took my hand and directed me to come along, but whatever it was it made a profound and lasting impression on me.

So to my grandma's question I obediently replied, "Yes, Grandma."

The meal was great, and to my surprise the concert wasn't half bad. I'm not saying I totally enjoyed the high-brow music or that I would ever in my life choose to attend a concert on my own unless there was absolutely nothing else in the world to do, but I enjoyed spending the evening with my grandparents and was highly complimented for my excellent behavior. No doubt my grandparents remembered how I had behaved last time. Patti, of course, was a little angel.

"Can we go to another concert while we're here?" Patti asked, when we were driving back to the ranch.

I gave her my cool-it-kid-before-I-break-your-face look.

Patti stuck out her tongue at me.

Granddad looked at me and smiled.

Grandma said, "There are no more concerts scheduled this week, Patti. Your granddad and I have attended twenty-two of these marvelous events this year. The orchestra is so divine, don't you think? You and PJ will have to spend more time with us during the summer if you want to take in more concerts."

Our five days at the ranch went by so fast. I kept myself entertained all week by going horseback riding, reading comics, playing ping pong with my granddad: soaking in the hot tub, watching old movies on TV, and listening to my grandparents talk about the good old days. Who would've ever thought life on a ranch could be so much fun! Patti had a good time, too. We actually made it through the week without having any major tiffs, which both of us agreed was pretty amazing.

When we got off the plane, Dad and Mom were at the airport terminal to greet us, and Jezi had her own special greeting for all of us when we got to the van. At times like that, I thank God we don't have a German shepherd. Even so, we drove home with the windows rolled down.

I went back to school on Monday with none of my work done. I was supposed to complete a research paper for science on the background and history of some invention. I had a book report due, two pages of math, and twenty questions to answer for history. And so, remaining doggedly true to my character, I had procrastinated. Now self-chastisement was setting in and I was feeling remorseful. Fortunately Theresa came to my rescue. During English period Mr. Cooper excused Theresa to work on her speech.

"May I take PJ with me?" asked Theresa.

"Oooh! Go for it, PJ!" exclaimed Gus.

Theresa fairly came unglued. She marched over to Gus, took her famous Theresa stance with hands on the hips, and said, 'Listen, buster, I didn't mean it that way. For two cents I'd give you a fat lip."

"No, no, please. I'll be good, I promise," pleaded Gus, in mock sincerity.

Sensing an angry scene developing, I grabbed Theresa by the arm and led her out of the room. As we walked to the library together, I realized how my feelings toward Theresa had changed over the past few months. It's not that I have romantic feelings towards her. At least I didn't think they were romantic feelings. Actually. I probably wouldn't recognize a romantic feeling if one passed me on the street.

"Gus is such a creep." said Theresa.

"Aw, don't let him get to you. He doesn't mean anything by it. I've known Gus a long time and we're alike in lots of ways. Remember a few months ago? I was the one acting like a clown all the time and doing and saying things to make you mad. You have such a cute way of responding. I did those things to get your reaction. I kinda think Gus is doing the same thing," I said.

Theresa stared at me and I blushed.

We reported to Ms. Newman, the librarian, and she pointed to a couple of empty seats in an out-of-the-way area where we could study. Theresa went through the lines of her speech while I followed along with the script. It was apparent that she had spent a lot of time memorizing the lines during vacation.

"Wow, Theresa, you have this thing maxed out!" I exclaimed.

"Yeah, but I get so blamed nervous when I do it in front of the class. I forget the lines," she said.

"Don't worry, you'll do fine in the competition. My dad always used to tell me that performing in front of people you know is lots harder than performing for strangers. Why don't you go through it one more time and try to focus on expression and gestures," I suggested.

The second time was even better than the first. I complimented Theresa and assured her once more that she had nothing to worry about. As we approached the classroom I saw someone come out of the boys restroom and run toward the daycare room.

I went into the classroom quickly and approached Mr. Cooper who was seated at his desk.

"May I please use the restroom?" I asked.

"Your break is just ten minutes from now. Can't you wait?" he asked

"No, Sir, I gotta go," I said excitedly.

I did have to go, but not for the reason he assumed. Mr. Arnold, the custodian, was standing inside the restroom surveying the wall when I entered.

"Well, what do you know? Here comes my bathroom buddy," he said, sarcastically. "Didn't you finish the first time?"

I didn't respond.

The wall was a mess. Someone had used a black crayon to scribble all over it. There were small squiggles, large overlapping oblong circles, and lines drawn up and down.

"I just repainted the entire wall during vacation." said Mr. Arnold. He looked at me with frustration showing on his face.

"I'm sorry," I said, and turned and walked out of the restroom and back to class. I decided this was not the time to tell him, I had seen a small boy running from the restroom just minutes before. I felt good because I finally had zeroed in on a suspect.

Mrs. Moser, Theresa's mom, and my dad drove us to the speech meet on Friday. Gus, Sybil, Janelle, and I rode with my Dad so we could practice our puppet show on the way. Theresa, Amy, Maggie, Charity, Esperanza, and Mr. Cooper rode in Mrs. Moser's van. Traffic was heavy on the way as commuters hurried to work in the city, but we managed to arrive in Fremont early enough to stop for breakfast at McDonalds.

Everyone was nervous as we stood around waiting for the competition to begin. Mr. Cooper and Mrs. Moser were judges, but not in the rooms where any of us from John Mark Christian School were competing. We were directed to proceed to our pre-assigned rooms to begin the competition. My dad came with us to watch our performance. Once in the room, the head judge announced that one of the puppet team had not shown. There would be only two schools competing.

Gus looked quizzically at me, and said, "That means we will win either first or second place, dude."

"Duh!" exclaimed Janelle.

Our puppet team was scheduled to go first. As I was taking the puppets out of the suitcase I suddenly realized we had forgotten to load the stage which my dad had made for us. I whispered our plight to Janelle and together we walked over to face the head judge. Since the host school had no stage, we improvised by turning a large table over on its side and placing it on top of another one. Gus, Sybil, Janelle, and I crouched behind the table waiting for the judge to tell us to begin. When we finished, we returned to join the audience and watch the second puppet team, our competition. This group of six suave-looking eighth graders used an elaborately decorated ark as their stage. Their skit about Noah's Ark was clever and their puppets appeared to be homemade.

"We have first place made," Gus whispered to me.

I wasn't so sure.

CHAPTER NINETEEN

THE LAST SHALL BE FIRST

I can do all things through Christ who gives me strength.
— Philippians 4:13

After dining at the nearest Taco Bell restaurant, we returned to the middle school to hear the verdict. The awards assembly would not begin until 1 :30 and since we had driven such a long way, Mr. Cooper went to the judging arena to ask if anyone from our school had won. If no one in our group won a first place, we would not stay for the ceremony.

"Well, I have good news and I have bad news," responded Mr. Cooper with a Cheshire smile on his face. He opened wider the door to the van where we were sitting. "PJ, please turn the radio down so I can hear myself think."

"O.K., Mr. Cooper, we can take it. Lay all this news on me. What did I win?" asked Gus.

"I thought you'd never ask. First. the bad news. We can't leave yet because at least one of you won a first place trophy."

"Yes!" Janelle exclaimed.

I looked intently at Mr. Cooper, studying his facial expression and to see if he would look directly at whoever won the first place trophy. Janelle thought our puppet team was the winner. I kept quiet because I had a feeling the other puppet team outdid us. Besides, Amy was the most likely person from our school to win. Mr. Cooper wasn't giving anything away. There was no change in his facial expression, in the inflection of his voice, nor did he look at anyone in particular.

"The good news is that I was able to look through all of the ribbons which will be handed out to our group, and there wasn't a white ribbon in the bunch," stated Mr. Cooper. "I can see by your puzzled look, Gus, that you don't understand. Let me explain in English. You all placed either first or second in your respective competitions. Now, isn't that good news?"

We waited, but not too patiently, for the awards ceremony to begin. Awards for the puppet division were given first, so our lingering suspense came to an abrupt end. We placed second. Big deal! There was only one other puppet team. The first place winner in each division was required to perform for the audience. Gus, Sybil, and I tried very hard to be gracious losers. We just hung our heads and moped. Janelle, who wrote most of our script, seemed to take it the hardest. I was sitting beside her, and when she kept making sarcastic comments and claiming that the judges were biased, I gently prodded her with my elbow and told her to cool it. To my surprise, she did.

We waited expectantly as the announcer gave out third and then second place ribbons in Amy's category and let out a thunderous roar when he called Amy to the stage to recite "The Highwayman." Her performance was absolutely flawless. Charity, Esperanza, and Maggie won second place ribbons in their divisions. Theresa's group was last to receive awards.

Third place was announced. A chubby kid went forward to claim his ribbon.

Second place went to a tall, redheaded kid who looked like an overgrown Dennis the Menace.

Mr. Cooper had already told us that everyone in our group would receive a red or blue ribbon. I knew even before it was announced who the winner was, and without thinking, I jumped up, waving my arms, and yelled at the top of my lungs, "Praise the Lord." People were staring at me. Mr. Cooper scrunched down in his seat. My dad looked at the ceiling. Janelle yanked me back to the pew. The announcer stood dumbfounded for a moment, then looked directly at me and said, "Good idea, sonny, but let's award this last trophy first. Would Theresa Moser please come forward?"

We were amazed! The class had never heard Theresa do her speech perfectly. Portraying the role of a patient, matronly schoolmarm who gradually loses her cool because of the unruly kindergartners she teaches, Theresa didn't miss a beat. I was on my feet cheering and not feeling a bit self-conscious when she concluded her speech. Then I glanced around and noticed that not only was our group up but everyone in the entire auditorium was giving Theresa a standing ovation. Theresa, with tears streaming down her cheeks, took the trophy from the announcer and ran from the auditorium. I was poised to go after her when Janelle said, "I think she just wants to be alone, PJ."

Going home that night, I suddenly realized the year was almost over and the few remaining weeks of school would go by in a blur because there were so many things happening. A large group of kids from kindergarten through eighth grade were signed up to run the Big Sur 5K. The school with the largest percentage of runners would receive $1,000. Then the very next week practically the entire student body was scheduled to visit Great America as a reward for getting pledges for Super Scrub. Super Scrub was a humongous car wash conducted at many locations around the city. Most everyone at school worked hard to get the necessary pledges because it meant a day off from school and a free trip to Great America. Following the day at Great America, the junior high was scheduled to fly to Washington D.C. for five days. Eighth grade "Ditch Day", the graduation banquet, and the graduation ceremony would round out the year. I got so tired just thinking about all those things that I fell asleep in the back of the van and slept all the way home.

Kent called Saturday afternoon and asked me to meet him at the mall. I had other things to do but agreed to meet him almost as an unconscious act. Kent looked terrible. His hair was uncombed, he breathed out the stale odor of cigarette smoke, and the tattered cut-offs he was wearing were really short. It was hard for me to believe that this person sitting opposite me had been my very best friend ever since pre-school. I swallowed hard, and decided to do a lot of listening.

"PJ, say old buddy, how 'bout loaning me fifty bucks?" he asked.

"You gotta be kidding, Kent. I don't have fifty dollars. I wouldn't know what that much money looked like," I replied. "What do you need it for?"

"Come on, PJ. I know you've got it. I'll pay you back in a week, promise. You guys are going to Washington D.C. soon, so I know you've got lots of spending money saved. I'll pay you back, honest," he said, sounding desperate.

"You didn't answer my question. Why do you need it?" I asked again.

"I can't tell you, PJ, but I'm in a real jam. I gotta get the money today. Say, I'll sell you this watch for fifty dollars. It's worth a lot more than that," he said, pulling a diamond-studded men's Longines watch from his pocket.

I shook my head in disbelief. There was only one way Kent could come by a watch that valuable.

"Kent, nothing is so bad that you have to steal. Come on, why don't you level with me. Maybe together we can figure out what to do. Remember when we got into trouble in grade school, and together we always figured out what to do? Come on, man, I want to help you," I said.

"Yeah, sure, some help you are. You aren't even my friend any more. I thought I could depend on you, PJ."

Getting up to leave, Kent pushed back so hard on the chair that it crashed to the floor. He sprinted down the wide aisle of the mall weaving in and out of people as he gradually disappeared from sight.

It would do no good for me to go after him. I picked the chair up, went directly to my bike, and pedaled home. I wondered if Kent was having trouble with his brother again. Lord, what would you have me do to help Kent, I prayed. Kent's my friend. but I don't know what to do. Lord, If he's having problems with his brother, please intervene and cause there to be peace between them. Thank you for helping him, Lord.

Sunday was the big race day. I had never run a race on Sunday, but I rationalized that this race was for a good cause so the Lord would understand. Thirty-eight students from John Mark Christian School were signed up to run the Big Sur 5K. I figured our school had a good shot at winning the $1,000 prize. I had done some recruiting myself. I used my powers to coerce Janelle, Peggy, Sybil, Jon, and Lori to run. Parents and friends could sign up in the name of the school, too, so my mom signed up and Patti tagged along. Since the rules didn't say you had to run the entire race, they figured it would be a piece of cake to walk the 3.2 miles. Gus is such a couch potato he wouldn't even walk it. Miss Puffer had already let me know that she was running the marathon, so we would get credit as a school for her running and I wouldn't be competing with her. We stood in a little cluster waiting for the start of the race.

"I can't believe I let you talk me into this, PJ," Janelle said, covering up a big yawn. "I should be sleeping soundly in my nice comfy bed."

"You should be in church, you mean," said Lori.

"Just think of it as community service. That $1000 will buy lots of neat stuff for our school," I said.

"Is Miss Puffer really running the marathon?" asked Jon.

"Yeah, sure, and I'm glad she is. She nearly beat me in the last 5K I ran. Don't let her age fool you. She can move that bod pretty fast," I said.

"Let's all stay together for the whole race, no matter what," said Sybil.

The place was packed with hundreds of kids of all sizes and shapes. I had trained to run this race and I wanted to do well, but I felt obligated to stay with the gang I had talked into running.

"No way!" exclaimed Peggy. "I want to finish sometime before summer, and besides I'm going to try to keep up with my grandpa. He's eighty-one years old, but most of the time he beats me when I run with him."

"PJ, you don't need to stay with us either. I know you've trained for this race. Go for it, dude." said Jon.

Our starting point was the finish line for the Big Sur Marathon. The course would take us out just over one and a half miles to the ocean where we would turn and come back to the finish line. The starter welcomed all the runners and called out the names of all the schools participating. As each school name was announced, loud cheering erupted. Our yell was puny by comparison. I made up my mind to be content with the T-shirt I would receive for finishing the race.

Right out of the chute, we were required to climb a rather steep hill. I had started from a position towards the back of the pack but rapidly wove my way to a place from which I could at least see the front runners. We made a right turn off the main highway onto a dirt road and continued running on level ground until we reached the ocean. From there the road disappeared and we were running in thick sand on the beach along the ocean front. Finally. we left the beach and picked our way along a trail which led us back to the dirt road. I thought running in the sand was rough and I was breathing heavily to prove it, but the trail was worse because it required continually climbing and running in single-file lines. I saw Peggy and her granddad running about thirty yards ahead of me, and when I reached the dirt road, I accelerated to try to catch up with them. When Peggy and her granddad turned onto the highway, I was a mere five yards behind them. The hill I had labored up at the beginning of the race now stretched downward before me to the finish line. Surveying the scene before me, I knew there was no way I could catch the lead runners. My legs were hurting, I was breathing hard, and I couldn't even catch a girl who hadn't trained nearly as hard as I had and an eighty-one year old man. Right then I decided I was a total wimp, and it was time for me to quit kidding myself that I would ever be good at track.

As I approached the finish line, it seemed as if hundreds of spectators were lining the street on both sides yelling and screaming at the top of their lungs. A huge banner stretched across the roadway between two giant sequoia trees displayed the words BIG SUR MARATHON. Peggy and her granddad had no idea I was running right on their heels. My timing was perfect. About ten yards from the finish line I made my move and raced ahead of them waving my hands over my head as I passed under the banner. I did it, I beat an eighty-one year old man.

"Keep moving. Keep your place in line. Please tear off the bottom part of your bib number. Nice job, kid." she yelled as she collected my number." Are you okay?"

"Yeah, sure. I feel just great," I replied, breathing heavily and holding my sides.

Breaking all the rules about what not to do following a race, I grabbed a drink from the refreshment table, plopped down on the closest patch of grass I could find, and downed the ice cold liquid in a single gulp. Others from John Mark straggled in gradually and joined me. Everyone compared stories about what they had experienced during the race. Patti and my mom finished just as the awards ceremony was about to begin. News of the front runners in the marathon was constantly being broadcast through huge speakers set up around the area. Since the winner would cross the finish line in less than thirty minutes, awards for the 5K were given out quickly.

I surely didn't think I had run a fast race. I had been so intent on beating Peggy's granddad, I failed to note my time when I crossed the finish line. I was really surprised when Peggy's name was called with a winning time of 21:43. She came in second place in her division. Her granddad always won first because there was no one his age running. The announcer barked out the name of the third place winner in my division with a time of 24:06. I would either win a first or a second place medal. I held my breath as the announcer prepared to call the name of the second place winner.

CHAPTER TWENTY

WHAT A TRIP

And we know that all things work together for good to them that love God, to them who are the called according to his purpose.

— Romans 8:28

"Coming in first with a time of twenty-one minutes and thirty-four seconds, PJ Nichols from John Mark Christian School. PJ, please make your way up here," the announcer barked.

I did my usual grandstanding as I waltzed forward to receive my medal. Miss Big Sur draped the red, white, and blue ribbon with the medal dangling at the end around my neck and gave me a big hug. She smiled and I spontaneously kissed her on the cheek. The crowd loved it. The young lady turned red. I took a bow, turned, and hotfooted it back to our group. We would not learn which school won the $1,000 prize for the highest percentage of runners until later.

Many of us went out for breakfast following the 5K awards. I would've enjoyed being at the finish line when Miss Puffer came across, but she would not be finishing the marathon for another three hours and I had lots of packing to do.

That very evening, my parents drove Gus, Jon, Billy, and me to the airport where we met the rest of our group in preparation for the flight to Washington D.C. We were flying the "Red Eye" flight out at 12:05 a.m., supposedly to save money. I really believe Mr. Cramer planned it that way because he thought we would sleep all the way and be less trouble for the stewardesses and all the other travelers. Wrong!

Mr. Cramer was at the airport to see us off, but he was not accompanying us to D.C. All of us were relieved when we learned that Mr. Cooper, not Mr. Bakker, was to be in charge of us on the trip. The girls would answer to Miss Puffer. who had been released from teaching duties to make the trip. She must've had her bags packed in advance, and although she walked rather stiffly, you would never know she had run twenty-six miles just hours before. Farewells and goodbyes were said to our parents, and then Mr. Cooper led the promenade from the terminal to our boarding gate. That very first venture should have been an omen to me of things to come on the trip.

Mr. Bakker, who was bringing up the rear of the procession, suddenly yelled out, "Wait a minute! Gus isn't here. Has anyone seen Gus?"

I was walking with Theresa and Tanya directly in front of Mr. Bakker. I dropped my bag, covered my ears, and grimaced.

"We don't need your silly antics, PJ," yelled Mr. Bakker. "This is serious. Gus was at the terminal when we checked our luggage. Come with me, PJ. Let's see if we can find him."

"Shouldn't we tell Mr. Cooper we're leaving the group?" I asked.

"Let me worry about Mr. Cooper," he said rather sarcastically.

Mr. Bakker and I backtracked to the terminal we had just left where we split up to search every nook and cranny. I went into a men's room and called out, "Gus, are you in here?"

Several voices responded simultaneously from behind stall doors, "Yeah, I'm over here."

Another voice yelled, "It's over. Go away, sweety. I don't want to party anymore. Oh, boo hoo!"

I got out of there so fast you would've thought I had been shot out of a cannon.

I had a queasy feeling in my stomach. On the mirror in that

restroom, drawn in the same exact way as the sketch on the wall at school was a peace sign with the initials JMCS97 underneath. I thought about going back to check the writing out more thoroughly but decided against it.

"Over here, PJ," Mr. Bakker called.

I turned and saw Mr. Bakker with Gus coming towards me. I fell in step with Gus who was walking slightly behind Mr. Bakker. Gus didn't say a word, but I could tell from his countenance that he had been severely chastised. I didn't say anything either because I was still trying to deal with the writing on the wall in that restroom. Of course, I thought Gus had done it, and if that airport restroom mirror, then probably the wall at school too. What else could I think? I quickly put the thought out of my mind.

When we arrived at the gate, Mr. Cooper had already handed out the boarding passes. Since there were only three remaining seats, Gus and I would be sitting with Mr. Bakker all the way to D.C.

Mr. Bakker was trying to tell Mr. Cooper about Gus when Lori and Tanya darted past them.

"Excuse me, girls," said Mr. Bakker, "but where do you think you are going?"

"Excuse me. Sir, but Miss Puffer said we could go shop around at the gift shop," said Lori.

"You don't have time to go shopping now, girls," responded Mr. Bakker. "Our plane will be boarding in a few minutes."

"But, Miss Puffer said . . . "

"Sorry, girls, it'll have to wait," interrupted Mr. Bakker.

Lori and Tanya looked at Mr. Cooper for support but didn't get any.

A few minutes later the flight attendant began boarding us. I guess the next incident shouldn't have surprised me too much. A stewardess informed Mr. Bakker that two seats assigned to our party were unoccupied. Gus and I, seated next to Mr. Bakker, cringed as he bolted from his seat and stormed down the aisle making a count of all the kids in our group. About that time Lori and Tanya came waltzing down the aisle and plopped into their assigned seats just ahead of Mr. Bakker and obviously oblivious to what was happening.

Mr. Bakker threw up his hands and said, "I'll deal with you later, girls." He huffed back down the aisle and made Gus move so that he could have the seat next to the aisle.

And then there was incident #3.

We were all dead tired by Monday afternoon after a sleepless night and after traipsing around Washington D.C. all day. The tour bus picked us up at the airport and took us to the Treasury Building where we stood in line for over an hour and then walked through a building where large sheets of money were printed. We had lunch and headed for the Walter Reed Hospital and Museum, which turned out to be a major disaster. The place was totally boring in the first place, but then our bus broke down and we were stuck there for over two hours. A truck was dispatched to repair the bus, but the truck had a flat tire on the way. Then, the tour director decided to call taxis for us to ride in to the hotel which was across town. So, a parade of ten taxi cabs came along. Let me tell you, the place looked like a zoo. It started to rain. There was no place to go to get out of the rain because the Walter Reed Museum had long since closed. It was getting dark. Some of the cabs were late. Some of the drivers couldn't speak English. Luggage was crammed into the trunk of the lead cab and five girls piled in, but then the driver couldn't get the cab started. The street was narrow, and with the bus blocking one side of the roadway, none of the other cabs could navigate around the lead cab. Tempers were getting short, primarily due to a total lack of sleep, and also because we were hungry and soaking wet. Finally, the lead cab was pushed out of the way, and two hours later we arrived at our hotel. The fantastic dinner planned for us in the hotel dining room ended up being a burger and cold. soggy fries at 1:00 a.m.

All in all, I had a fun time in Washington. Our tour guide was a little loony, but he kept us entertained while we traveled around the city visiting the various historical places. Every place we went, Lori would asked, "Excuse me, but is there a shopping mall nearby?" The tour guide's answer to all questions was, "A lot of things depend on a lot of things." I shared a room with Billy, Dirk, and Jose. Billy returned to the hotel every night loaded down with trinkets, toys, and junk which the teachers gradually confiscated because he kept doing dumb things like shooting plastic darts at girls, squirting water from a supersoaker on people, or turning on a beeper at totally inappropriate times. Mr. Cramer made the room arrangements to purposely separate the eighth grade boys, but he told our parents it was because he wanted us to be a positive influence on the seventh graders. That's a laugh. Those guys were so immature. I spent so much time visiting with the security guard who was stationed in the hallway that we became best friends. The girls did their share of getting into mischief, too. Diana and Cheryl manipulated the window in their room so that it opened wide enough for them to lean way out and talk to each other at all hours of the night. Miss Puffer didn't find out about that until the last night when she happened to be walking by the pool, looked up, and saw all these bodies leaning out windows up on the fifteenth floor carrying on conversations and planning secret rendezvous.

The most fun I had on the entire trip also happened on the last night. We had spent the day touring the memorials and the Smithsonian Institute, returned to the hotel to clean up, and then boarded the bus again to attend what we had envisioned to be a dull, boring play. We saw a Gilbert and Sullivan play called "The Pirates of Penzance" and ate the best meal I've ever had in my life. All the way to the play, the tour guide kept telling us we would be seeing a play about a pirate with no pants and that the meal would be cold pasta and garlic bread. We were dressed up in our Sunday best, and although we were extremely tired from our long week with little sleep, we were poised to make the most of what promised to be a dull evening.

I was seated at a table with Maggie, Sandra, Kristina, and Gus. The play was incredible. The actors and actresses were totally cool. Maggie fell in love with one dude who danced right in front of our table and knelt at her feet. He took a sip of her coke and fell over as if dead. Little did he know that her coke had been generously doctored with salt. He revived, sat up, kissed Maggie's hand. and whispered that she made a mean drink. It was like a three-ring circus with stuff going on all over the stage and in the audience. Our group was the last one to leave that evening because all the girls had to get autographs and swoon over the actors.

Continuing true to form for the entire week, it was after 1:00 a.m. when we finally checked into our rooms. I thought my friend, the security guard, was going to cry when I came out to complain that the guys next door were banging on the wall. I figured he was just sad because we would be checking out in a few hours. We shook hands and I returned to find myself locked out of my room. I was standing in the hall banging on the door dressed in my short white pjs with red rhinos on them when Theresa opened the door.

"What do you want, PJ?" she asked.

"Oh my gosh," I exclaimed. "I have the wrong room."

"Sure you do! You're just trying to keep me from getting my beauty sleep," she said. rubbing her eyes. She looked so funny standing there in her bunny slippers and wearing a long shirt-type gown with Garfield on it . Her hair was up in some sort of net thing, and this white gunk was all over her face.

"No comment," I said, retreating quickly in the opposite direction.

My friend, the security guard, laughed and shook his head. "You two make a fine-looking pair," he said.

The next morning we were up at 6:00 a.m. and had breakfast on the bus at 7 00 as we journeyed to Mt. Vernon to visit George Washington's homestead. With all the things to do and places to see, Lori still spent most of her time in the gift shop. She had to buy an extra bag just to cart all the stuff she bought on the trip back home. Some of us were so tired we plopped down on the grass outside the gift shop and waited for our tour guide to return.

"I gotta go potty," said Gus.

"Be my guest," I remarked.

"But where's the bathroom around this place?" asked Gus. "I haven't seen one all morning."

"You mean you haven't visited the privies, Gus? Why, I sat on the very privy Martha Washington used," said Maggie, laughing.

"What're you talking about, girl?" asked Gus.

I laughed so hard my sides hurt.

"You see that little brick building right over there, Gus? That, my friend, is a bathroom. They called them privies in George Washington's day and there were separate ones for the family and for the servants," I said.

Gus got so mad I thought he was going to start a fight with me, but he stormed off saying, "Aw, you sound like a tour guide, PJ. I'm in no mood to listen to your gibberish about outhouses. You guys can privy if you want. I'm going to find a tree."

From Mt. Vernon we went to a railroad station which had been converted into a beautiful mall. Lori, our perennial shopper, should have been in hog heaven, but she lamented, "Here we are in the mother of all malls and I've spent all my money."

Billy was so naive he paid twenty dollars for a hat with a marijuana cluster and was wearing it when Mr. Bakker walked over and snatched it from his head. Mr. Bakker was so angry he stuffed the hat into the nearest trash can and proceeded to lecture Billy in front of hundreds of people milling about. Poor Billy was in tears and out twenty dollars, and the saddest part of the whole deal is that I don't think Billy understood what was happening.

Mr. Cooper gave us specific instructions to return to our tour bus by 4:00 p.m. so that we would have plenty of time to get to the airport. The year before. some boy got separated from his partner in the mall and no one could find him. After searching for two hours and just when calling the police was the next viable option, they found the boy sitting on a bench outside the mall. Our group had made it through five days without losing anyone, but when it really counted and we were pressed for time Peggy, Maggie, and Kristina failed to show up. Mr. Cooper and Mr. Bakker were standing outside the bus arguing about what to do. Mr. Bakker came right out and told Mr. Cooper it was his fault because he had been too lenient with us all week. Mr. Cooper very calmly informed him that he needed to trust God and quit trying to run things his own way. Some of us felt like clapping and yelling out our support for Mr. Cooper, but fortunately the seriousness and mood of the moment persuaded us to remain silent.

Mr. Bakker slung his backpack over his back and stormed onto the bus, sat down on the front seat, and put his head in his hands.

At 4:10 p.m. Mr. Cooper, who had been conferring with the tour guide, got on the bus and said, “We’ll wait five more minutes and then send all the adults out to search for the girls. If they don’t show up, we’ll have to notify the police and leave without them, or miss our plane.”

What a trip this has been, I thought.

CHAPTER TWENTY-ONE

THE END IS NEAR

The Lord is my shepherd, I shall lack nothing. He makes me lie down in green pastures, he leads me beside quiet waters, he restores my soul.

— Psalm 23: 13

Peggy, Maggie and Kristina darted through traffic as they crossed in the middle of the street. An angry driver slammed on his brakes, sat on his horn, stuck his head out the window yelling unpleasantries at the girls, and burned rubber after they cleared the roadway.

"We got lost," Maggie huffed, all out of breath.

"I was so scared," said Peggy.

"Yeah, these creepy dudes were chasing us, and . . . "

"Enough, girls. Just go . . . get on the bus now!" exclaimed Mr. Cooper, who had been standing outside the bus watching for the girls. "Let's go, Pete," he said to the driver. "We have a plane to catch."

Mr. Cooper smiled and rolled his eyes upwards as he walked past me.

Somehow I figured the worst might be yet to come, so I tagged along close to Mr. Cooper when our bags were being checked and processed through security.

The buzzer sounded when Billy stepped through. We had been

counseled about the seriousness of airport security which made what Billy did even more serious. The contents which Billy emptied into the tray revealed a set of handcuffs, a foldout comb that looked like a knife with a long blade, three miniature darts in a case, and miscellaneous other gadgets. The security guard shook his head and called for our leader. Mr. Cooper told Mr. Bakker and Miss Puffer to take everyone to the boarding area while he resolved the issue with a not-too-pleasant guard. We learned later that many of the items Billy had were confiscated and would not be returned.

Tempers were short, everyone was zonked out, and no one was taking anything off of anyone. If Miss Puffer had not intervened Stan and Dirk would've been throwing punches. When Mr. Cooper started passing out the boarding passes, I asked him if I could sit by him. He gave me a quizzical look, but said he guessed he could allow that as long as I didn't snore.

Kent had been on my mind a lot all during the week, and I just couldn't hold it in any longer.

"Mr. Cooper, do you remember the time we talked about suicide during Bible study?" I asked.

"Well, vaguely, PJ. Refresh my memory. Is something bothering you about what I said?" he asked.

"No, not about what you said, but I'm afraid a friend of mine might try something stupid," I said.

"You're afraid a friend of yours might try to commit suicide? Is it someone on this trip with us?" asked Mr. Cooper.

"No, Sir. It's not someone who goes to JMCS. I don't think I should tell his name," I said.

"PJ, if this person is truly thinking about committing suicide, friend or not, you need to tell someone about it so he can get help before it's too late. I seem to remember that you were the one who raised the issue before. Am I correct?"

"Yes, Sir, I guess so. I just feel like I would be betraying a confidence if I told."

"I want to share something with you that I haven't told anyone at school except Mr. Cramer, PJ. I think the time is right, and I need to share both with you and if the opportunity permits, even with the class before you all graduate. I've been working through the tragedy of my son's death, and it has been extremely hard to deal with. My son died around 9:00 p.m. while on duty as a security guard. At first the police thought it was a homicide, but then the final report from the coroner's office stated that he committed suicide with his own gun while sitting in his car."

Mr. Cooper paused, stared out the window, and then continued.

"It has been hard for me to accept Danny's death as a suicide. He had too much going for him. I had talked to him just two days before he died, and while there was no indication that anything was wrong, the last thing he said was so strange. He said, 'Dad?' in the form of a question and paused, and when I said, 'Yes. Danny, what is it?' he said, 'I just want you to know I love you. I know I haven't told you before, but I really love you and thank you for everything you've done for me.' He didn't leave a note, he paid his rent before he went to work that day, and he even had tickets to a baseball game in his wallet. He loved baseball. I will always wonder if he was struggling with something he just couldn't bring himself to share with me."

I sat in silence listening to this man pour out his love for his son, but I didn't know what to say. After a brief silence, Mr. Cooper continued.

"PJ, you can't remain silent. I have to face the hard reality that my son committed suicide, and I failed to see the signs or listen when he was calling out for help. You need to share what you know with your parents or Pastor Bob. People who talk about committing suicide will often do the deed. There are usually indications that a person is contemplating suicide . . . like depression, feeling sorry for one's self, or talking about it like your friend did. Just don't wait too long, PJ."

"I tried telling once before when Kent . . . " I covered my mouth realizing what I had said.

"It's okay. I had a feeling you were talking about Kent," said Mr. Cooper.

We talked some more but basically we left it at that. I knew what I had to do when I got home.

✥

School was boring as ever, but at least the end was in sight. By math time, I was already in over my head with projects assigned before the D.C. trip which I had not done and was getting more and more frustrated with the work Mr. Bakker was piling on us. So, I decided it was time to visit the restroom. For once I was making a legitimate visit, too. I jaunted merrily down the corridor humming the tune to the chorus "In My Heart, Lord, Be Glorified" and pushed open the door to the restroom with much more force than I intended. I really had to go. I had become so accustomed to the routine of playing sleuth that when I finally came face to face with the culprit I didn't have the foggiest idea what to do.

Quickly regaining my composure, I said with as much authority in my high-pitched voice as I could muster, "So, Billy, are you making a career of doing restroom walls?"

Billy had backed up from the wall, dropping the marker he had been using. Neatly penned in the all-too-familiar style were the words:

I'M BACK, SUCKER.

Evidently he was in the process of drawing a peace sign as it appeared half finished under the words when I interrupted.

"PJ, please don't tell on me. You're not going to tell, are you, ol' buddy? I'll make a deal with you. You can come over to my house, and I'll give you some of the neat things I got on the trip. How 'bout it?" he asked.

I had known Billy for a long time. Never would I have suspected him. Over the last few months I had suspected Dirk, a kindergarten kid, the fifth grade girl I caught going into the restroom, Gus, and even Mr. Arnold, but never Billy. It was all so logical though. One day a week for as long as I could remember Billy has been coming to school two hours late. He told us he had to sit in a whirlpool to strengthen his legs after an accident. Billy, not being a close friend of mine, had never told me about the accident. He had the perfect opportunity to scribble on restroom walls. As I remembered the dumb stunts he pulled on our trip, it also dawned on me that he often demonstrated a lack of maturity and was capable of doing something as childish as writing on walls.

"Sorry, Billy, no deal," I said. "You need help, buddy." And I walked out leaving him standing there.

I missed eighth grade "Ditch Day" when the class went to Great America because I had a stomach virus, but Gus filled me in on the details. After I reported Billy's capers to Mr. Cramer, my mom came to get me and I spent the next two days traveling between the bed and the bathroom, if you know what I mean. No one knew why Billy didn't go to Great America, but I knew and kept it to myself.

Friday afternoon I was feeling better so I rode my bike over to Kent's house. As I approached his house, the usual loud rock music was not blaring from the second floor. I leaned my bike against the wall toward the back of the house and walked around the corner to knock on the back door. Kent was sitting on the steps with his head in his lap and with his hands out of sight under his legs. He definitely wasn't expecting company.

"Hi, Kent," I said. "How's it going?"

Kent looked up at me with tears streaming down his cheeks, shook his head, and took his hands out from under his legs. He held a large pistol in his right hand, waving it back and forth.

The thought passed through my mind that he was going to shoot me, so I instinctively moved backwards.

"I just can't do it, PJ. I've been sitting here for hours trying to think of just one reason to keep on living. I can't think of any reasons, but I haven't got the guts to pull the trigger," Kent stammered.

"Praise the Lord! Kent, you do have a reason to live. God loves you and wants you to live for Him. Don't you see, He has given you the good sense not to pull the trigger." I reasoned. I wanted to take the gun from Kent, or at least get him to put it down. but I hesitated.

Without even looking down, Kent placed the gun on the step. I wondered if it was really loaded. He kind of laughed through the tears and said, "Yeah, that's what you always tell me. PJ. Show me! Just show me how God could love something as awful as me."

Boy, talk about being put on the spot. There I was face to face with a guy who was inches from committing suicide, staring at a .357 Magnum on the step between us, and not knowing what I could say to convince him that God would help him. Yeah, sure, I talk the talk, but what could I do when it really mattered. I put my arm around Kent and with my other hand took the gun from the step and placed it on the other side of me. Taking a deep breath, I silently asked God for help.

"Kent, I know you don't want to hear what I have to say, but please listen. There is someone who can help you. Will you just listen to me this time, please?" I asked.

I felt that God was opening the door a little when Kent humbly said, "Okay, PJ, I'll listen. Things can't get any worse."

The gun was resting on the edge of the step and I eased it off hoping the sound of it hitting the ground wouldn't distract Kent as I told him about Mr. Cooper's son. As I retold the story he had shared with me, I found myself crying. I was crying because of the tremendous impact that story had on me, because Kent was my friend and because I was so afraid I had waited too long. I was afraid there was nothing I could do or say at this point to convince him that suicide was not the answer.

When I finished, Kent looked me squarely in the eyes and said, "So, PJ, what can I do? I can't go on living in this house. My mother sleeps around, my brothers beat me up, there's no money, and I'm in trouble with the police."

"You have to let someone help you, Kent. Will you come with me to talk to Pastor Bob? Things are never so bad that you should take your life. There is always more than one way to solve a problem, and God gave us people like Pastor Bob to help. Come on, let's go," I said, getting up to show him I meant it.

To my surprise, Kent followed me. We rode our bikes in silence to John Mark Christian School and walked into the church offices which are located on the same property. I knew God was with us when the secretary said Pastor Bob was in his office. My dad calls these kind of situations divine appointments. I was convinced it was so when the secretary took us right in to see Pastor Bob. He listened as I explained the situation to him, prayed with us, and after a short while said, "PJ, I need to talk with Kent alone. Thank you for bringing him to me. Are you okay with that. Kent?"

"Sure, that's okay," he said. "Thanks, PJ. You probably saved my life."

I nodded my head and left the office. The sky was the bluest blue I think I have ever seen when I walked out of the office and looked up to thank God. I was leaning against the wall when Mrs. Moser drove onto the parking lot and honked at me. A familiar-looking gorilla puppet and the ugly guy we had used at the speech competition were framed in the window in the back seat. Adam, my gorilla puppet, and Eve, his blonde friend, were going through all sorts of silly antics, many of which I had done with Adam a few months before when I first met Theresa. I wondered why my puppets were hitching a ride with Mrs. Moser. As she rolled past, the gorilla shifted to the rear window still gyrating and acting stupid. When Mrs. Moser parked the station wagon near the school auditorium, Theresa and Lori piled out of the back and ran towards me.

Not now, Lord, I need to do something about that gun.

EPILOGUE

But those who hope in the LORD will renew their strength. They will soar on wings like eagles: they will run and not grow weary, they will walk and not be faint.
—Isaiah 40 31

"Did you like our puppet show?" asked Theresa.

"Oh it has potential. Seems like I saw some of that act before," I said giving her my best smile. "What are you doing with the puppets, anyway?"

"We just finished doing a puppet show for a pre-school," said Lori.

"Yeah, and we were returning the puppets to Pastor Bob, but since you're here you may take them back," she said.

I walked with the girls to the car where they helped me load the puppets into Theresa's backpack. I promised to return it to her on Monday and was on my way.

I pedaled quickly to Kent's house, threw my bike down on the grass, and ran to the back to find the gun. Dark shadows cast by the trees and the house enveloped the backyard. Apparently no one was home. Throwing the backpack down I crawled under the steps on my hands and knees, retrieved the gun, and backed out the same way I had crawled in. The safety was on, but I didn't want to take any chances. I removed the clip and checked the chamber to be sure no shells were lodged there. Then I placed the gun as far down into the backpack as it would go and pedaled home. My mom turned three shades of blue when I took the gun from the backpack. After I explained the situation, she took the gun and placed it in a locked closet until Dad came home. I would tell you about what happened with that .357 Magnum, but that's a whole story by itself.

Theresa finished her song, and I was jolted back to the present when I heard Mr. Cramer introducing the valedictorian and salutatorian for the graduating class of John Mark Christian School.

"It is my pleasure to present to you Peter Jonathan Nichols III. PJ as he is affectionately known around here, the salutatorian of our graduating class." announced Mr. Cramer.

My classmates cheered as I walked somberly toward the podium.

Mr. Cooper and Miss Puffer stood and applauded, sheepishly looked around and quickly sat back down.

My dad cried; however, I didn't know about that until later when we went out for dinner and my mom told me. She also instructed me not to let my dad know that she had seen him crying.

Quite poised and totally in control, I welcomed the school board, Pastor, Pastor Bob, Mr. Cramer, teachers, parents, and all the guests to our graduation. Then I turned and planted a juicy kiss on Mr. Cramer's cheek before returning to my seat.

Once again, my classmates were on their feet hooting and hollering.

The prim, matronly president of the school board, who was sitting on the stage to present diplomas, was totally shocked.

My dad covered his face with his hands.

Patti giggled uncontrollably.

Mr. Cramer followed me to my seat and gave me a big bear hug.

When it was announced a week before graduation that I was to be the salutatorian, many kids in my class were shocked, but Mr. Cramer, Mr. Cooper, and my parents weren't. They believed in me and helped me to realize I could be funny without being the class clown. I could make good grades without being pompous, I could be a leader instead of a follower, and I had proven by my actions that Christ lives in my heart and not just in my head.

Mr. Cramer returned to the podium and said, "And now on a more serious note (I hope) it is my pleasure to present to you Miss Theresa Moser, the valedictorian of our graduating class."

Theresa's speech had it all. The audience laughed at her humor, some kids in our class cried when she shared the difficulties she had faced and overcome, and she brought all of us to our feet when she talked about the influence Mr. Cooper had on her life. I didn't know anyone ever received a standing ovation for a graduation speech, but Theresa did.

Next, each one of us individually had to stand on the stage while Mr. Cramer roasted us. He used the information we had written about ourselves where we talked about our likes and dislikes, goals, favorite teacher, favorite class, and some stuff he must've wrenched from our parents. Overall, it was a fun time. The audience really laughed when he read the part I wrote about the Washington D.C. trip. I merely said that the security guard was the best part of the trip. None of us knew what anyone else in the class had written because the papers were collected as we finished, but it was amazing to listen to the comments made about Mr. Cooper. I knew he had made a huge impact on my life, but I was stunned when more than half the class responded in the same manner.

After we received our diplomas, we egressed from the auditorium into the school cafeteria for refreshments. Theresa and I were first in line leading the rest of the class down the aisle. The room was colorfully decorated with blue and white balloons and streamers, a large banner offered congratulations to the graduating class, and one wall was totally covered with a collage of pictures of our life from babyhood to teenager. Theresa turned to face me with tears rolling down her cheeks. Without saying a word, we hugged, and she was gone. Theresa is going to South High next year, so I'm sure our paths will cross many times.

As I milled about the room shaking hands, hugging the girls, and receiving complimentary pats on the back from former teachers who shook their heads in wonder, I came face to face with Kent.

Kent spoke first. "Congratulations, ol' buddy. You made it!"

"Yeah, can you believe it? I really hate to leave this place. We spent a lot of good years here, Kent," I said.

"Yes, we did, and then I blew it. I tried to blame all my problems on my family, but Pastor Bob has helped me to see that no matter how bad my family situation might be, I can overcome it with God's help. I would've been on that stage with you if only I had listened to Mr. Cramer and Pastor Bob earlier. And you," Kent added.

"So, what are you going to do now?" I asked.

"Well, I'm staying with Pastor Bob for the time being. He thinks there's hope for me," smiled Kent. "I'm going with Pastor Bob to Hume Lake this summer to work. This fall I'll be going to South High just like you and all my buddies here at JMCS."

"All right, dude, that's awesome!" I exclaimed, giving him a high-five.

Patti and my parents surrounded me and led me to the door.

"Let's go celebrate," said my dad.

"Yeah. Let's go to Taco Bell!" exclaimed Patti.

As we were walking to the van, I heard Mr. Cooper talking with some parents about the junior high. Always the teacher, I thought.